Celebrating Sunday for Catholic Families 2016–2017

Patricia J. Hughes

Nihil Obstat
Very Reverend Daniel A. Smilanic, JCD
Vicar for Canonical Services
Archdiocese of Chicago
September 29, 2015

Imprimatur
Reverend Monsignor Ronald A. Hicks
Vicar General
Archdiocese of Chicago
September 29, 2015

The *Nihil Obstat* and *Imprimatur* are declarations that the material is free from doctrinal or moral error and is granted permission to publish in accordance with c. 827. No legal responsibility is assumed by the grant of this permission. No implication is contained herein that those who have granted the *Nihil Obstat* or *Imprimatur* agree with the content, opinions, or statements expressed.

As a publisher, LTP works toward responsible stewardship of the environment. Visit www.LTP.org/environment to learn more about how this book was manufactured.

CELEBRATING SUNDAY FOR CATHOLIC FAMILIES 2016–2017 © 2016 Archdiocese of Chicago: Liturgy Training Publications, 3949 South Racine Avenue, Chicago IL 60609. Phone 1-800-933-1800; fax: 1-800-933-7094; e-mail orders@ltp.org; website www.LTP.org. All rights reserved.

ISBN: 978-1-61671-263-1

CSCF17

"You shall love the LORD your God with all your heart, and with all your soul, and with all your might. Keep these words that I am commanding to you today in your heart. Recite them to your children and talk about them when you are at home and when you are away, when you lie down and when you rise."

(Deuteronomy 6:5–7)

Contents

How to Use
Celebrating Sunday for Catholic Families

This small weekly guide draws on the Gospel for each Sunday and Holyday for the coming year. It is intended to help parents engage their children with the Mass and deepen their appreciation of the richness of their faith life. So often, going to Mass becomes a weekly event that begins and ends at the church door. The brief reflection for the parent on an excerpt from the Gospel is intended to spark his or her thinking about the Scripture that will lead to conversation with the family on the way to and from Mass. Suggestions for questions and conversation starters are provided, as well as some practice or practical way to carry this reflection into the life of the family.

We hope that many of the reflections and suggestions will enrich your family's life of faith. Some weeks, you may have other needs, concerns, or ideas that fit your life. If so, engage your children with those. A note about very young children: they are very able to enter into the liturgy through their senses. Singing the hymns, calling their attention to the changing colors of the liturgical seasons, and sitting where they can observe the gestures of the Mass are all ways to form them in the faith. Always remember, as the Rite of Baptism proclaims, you, as parents, are your children's first and most important teachers.

September 4, 2016

Twenty-Third Sunday in Ordinary Time

Hearing the Word

Luke 14:25–33

In the name of the Father, and of the Son, and of the Holy Spirit.

Great crowds were traveling with Jesus, and he turned and addressed them, "If anyone comes to me without hating his father and mother, wife and children, brothers and sisters, and even his own life, he cannot be my disciple. Whoever does not carry his own cross and come after me cannot be my disciple. Which of you wishing to construct a tower does not first sit down and calculate the cost to see if there is enough for its completion? Otherwise, after laying the foundation and finding himself unable to finish the work the onlookers should laugh at him and say, 'This one began to build but did not have the resources to finish.' Or what king marching into battle would not first sit down and decide whether with ten thousand troops he can successfully oppose another king advancing upon him with twenty thousand troops? But if not, while he is still far away, he will send a delegation to ask for peace terms. In the same way, any one of you who does not renounce all his possessions cannot be my disciple."

Reflecting on the Word

Jesus is teaching the difficult demands that involve being his disciple. When he speaks of "hating" relatives, he surely didn't mean this literally. We can think of this as creating some balance in loving, and not loving anything or anyone to the exclusion of loving God. In Semitic idiom, to "hate" means to "love less" rather than a lack of love. It isn't easy to be a disciple, and it takes giving up attachments to possessions as well as commitment.

...... ON THE WAY TO MASS:

Did you have to make any hard choices or decisions this week? How would a follower of Jesus choose?

ON THE WAY HOME FROM MASS: ......

Jesus said that it is not easy to be his disciple. What did you hear him say about making choices?

Living the Word

Write two or three petitions for family members to use as a mantra this week. In the morning or evening, coach each child in the mantra. Consider using the following: "When people try to get me in trouble . . . ," "When it's hard to be nice to someone else . . . ," and "When I'm asked to do something that's difficult . . . ." The response is always, "I will follow you, Jesus." Rehearse these each day, as prayer. Place a cross on the counter or a table, and mention daily that disciples choose the cross. Assure your children that they only need to ask, and Jesus will help them.

September 11, 2016

Twenty-Fourth Sunday in Ordinary Time

Hearing the Word

Luke 15:1–7

In the name of the Father, and of the Son, and of the Holy Spirit.

Tax collectors and sinners were all drawing near to listen to Jesus, but the Pharisees and scribes began to complain, saying, "This man welcomes sinners and eats with them." So to them he addressed this parable. "What man among you having a hundred sheep and losing one of them would not leave the ninety-nine in the desert and go after the one until he finds it? And when he does find it, he sets it on his shoulders with great joy and, upon his arrival home, he calls together his friends and neighbors and says to them, 'Rejoice with me because I have found my lost sheep.' I tell you, in just the same way there will be more joy in heaven over one sinner who repents than over ninety-nine righteous people who have no need of repentance."

Reflecting on the Word

When the scribes and Pharisees complain that Jesus eats with sinners, Jesus demonstrates through parables that God loves the sinner who repents. In the shepherd who found his sheep, Jesus portrays an understanding God. It is no surprise that Jesus' critics do not understand that saving what is lost causes more rejoicing than simple faithfulness. God is merciful to those who return yet supportive of those who are already true followers.

...... ON THE WAY TO MASS:

We trust Jesus to guide us when we seem to be lost. What do you remember about being lost and then found?

ON THE WAY HOME FROM MASS: ......

If you lost something really important to you, what would you do to find it? Would you pray about it?

Living the Word

This Gospel is a prime opportunity to plan a family trip for the Sacrament of Penance, and then to share in rejoicing with a meal out, a special movie at home, or a walk through a park or a museum. The point is to experience God's mercy and then to celebrate. For preschoolers, hide a lamb cutout (cookie?) or a coin (quarters in foil?) in the house or yard, and let the hunt begin. Remind the children that God always welcomes sinners back.

September 18, 2016

Twenty-Fifth Sunday in Ordinary Time

Hearing the Word

Luke 16:10–13

In the name of the Father, and of the Son, and of the Holy Spirit.

Jesus said to his disciples, "The person who is trustworthy in very small matters is also trustworthy in great ones; and the person who is dishonest in very small matters is also dishonest in great ones. If, therefore, you are not trustworthy with dishonest wealth, who will trust you with true wealth? If you are not trustworthy with what belongs to another, who will give you what is yours? No servant can serve two masters. He will either hate one and love the other, or be devoted to one and despise the other. You cannot serve both God and mammon."

Reflecting on the Word

Proclaiming this Gospel (Luke 16:10–13) in its longer form will add clarity to the parable. This story seems to raise questions, but the most important point is in the last line. We read, "You cannot serve both God and mammon." In other words, you cannot be dishonest in your dealings and still hope to serve God adequately. This Gospel seems to say that money should not be the complete focus of our attention. Do we confuse our dependence on money for our needs with dependence on money for happiness? Life without God is empty.

...... ON THE WAY TO MASS:

I wonder what life would be like if we had all of the money we ever wanted.

ON THE WAY HOME FROM MASS: ......

How can we live in today's world, and balance a desire for material goods with a desire to be a good disciple of Jesus?

Living the Word

Pope Francis' encyclical Laudato Si' makes it clear that we are responsible for the environment. Take fifteen minutes with each family member and walk around the house, the school, or the neighborhood to discover some ways that you can care for the world around you. Small discoveries can lead to good habits and may lead to developing the "ecological spirituality" that Pope Francis speaks of in his encyclical. What do we waste, and what should we save? Where do we find God in our surroundings? God has given us a beautiful world. How do we cherish what God has provided?

September 25, 2016

Twenty-Sixth Sunday in Ordinary Time

Hearing the Word

Luke 16:19–25

In the name of the Father, and of the Son, and of the Holy Spirit.

Jesus said to the Pharisees: "There was a rich man who dressed in purple garments and fine linen and dined sumptuously each day. And lying at his door was a poor man named Lazarus, covered with sores, who would gladly have eaten his fill of the scraps that fell from the rich man's table. Dogs even used to come and lick his sores. When the poor man died, he was carried away by angels to the bosom of Abraham. The rich man also died and was buried, and from the netherworld, where he was in torment, he raised his eyes and saw Abraham far off and Lazarus at his side. And he cried out, 'Father Abraham, have pity on me. Send Lazarus to dip the tip of his finger in water and cool my tongue, for I am suffering torment in these flames.' Abraham replied, 'My child, remember that you received what was good during your lifetime while Lazarus likewise received what was bad; but now he is comforted here, whereas you are tormented."

Reflecting on the Word

The rich man in the Gospel valued his wealth to the exclusion of all else. He neglected both charity and social responsibility. The parable demonstrates how a situation can literally change overnight when Abraham, in the afterlife, refuses mercy to a rich man who rejected the needs of others during his earthly life. The description of justice may seem harsh, with Abraham as the spokesman, but the point of righteous living is clear. Lazarus gained God's heavenly mercy as reward for his suffering.

...... ON THE WAY TO MASS:

As disciples of Jesus, who are we responsible for? Is mercy required of us?

ON THE WAY HOME FROM MASS ......

Pope Francis declared a Jubilee Year of Mercy from December 8, 2015, to November 20, 2016. How do we act mercifully to our classmates and members or our family?

Living the Word

It's time for costumes and a play: one person will be the rich man, and the others portray Lazarus and Abraham (an alternative would be to enact the play with puppets). Read today's First Reading (Amos 6:1, 4–7) to the rich man. Invite your children to act out who was happy in life, and after the rich man dies, who was happy after death. Review with the children how Abraham figuratively shook his finger at the rich man in hell and reminded him that people on earth need to pay attention to the teachings of God. What could the rich man have done to make his life pleasing to God?

October 2, 2016

Twenty-Seventh Sunday in Ordinary Time

Hearing the Word

Luke 17:5–10

In the name of the Father, and of the Son, and of the Holy Spirit.

The apostles said to the Lord, "Increase our faith." The Lord replied, "If you have faith the size of a mustard seed, you would say to this mulberry tree, 'Be uprooted and planted in the sea,' and it would obey you.

"Who among you would say to your servant who has just come in from plowing or tending sheep in the field, 'Come here immediately and take your place at table'? Would he not rather say to him, 'Prepare something for me to eat. Put on your apron and wait on me while I eat and drink. You may eat and drink when I am finished'? Is he grateful to that servant because he did what was commanded? So should it be with you. When you have done all you have been commanded, say, 'We are unprofitable servants; we have done what we were obliged to do.'"

Reflecting on the Word

Jesus responds to the Apostles' request by pointing out that a tiny mustard seed grows to greatness, even though the magnificent mulberry tree has vast, deep roots. It only takes a small amount of faith, then, to accomplish great things. The Apostles don't necessarily need a vast, deep faith; they need a stronger faith. Jesus holds up the servant for admiration because the servant did all that was asked of him. Whether or not the servant was expected to cook and serve and plow is not as important as his clear discipleship, his "yes."

...... ON THE WAY TO MASS:

Do people sometimes ask you to do too many things? Does it seem unfair?

ON THE WAY HOME FROM MASS: ......

Jesus says today that a tiny amount of faith counts. Can you share a story of your mustard-seed faith?

Living the Word

Be prepared with a small sack of mustard seeds, and a small amount of apple and watermelon seeds. On a counter, spell out the word faith with each type of seed. Is "small seed faith" any less than "large seed faith"? Each example spells "faith" and means the same thing. Share the Apostles' Creed each morning, afternoon, or evening during the coming week. This prayer is a way to celebrate and name what we believe, in faith. Remind the family that faith is a gift from God.

October 9, 2016

Twenty-Eighth Sunday in Ordinary Time

Hearing the Word

Luke 17:11–19

In the name of the Father, and of the Son, and of the Holy Spirit.

As Jesus continued his journey to Jerusalem, he traveled through Samaria and Galilee. As he was entering a village, ten lepers met him. They stood at a distance from him and raised their voices saying, "Jesus, Master! Have pity on us!" And when he saw them, he said, "Go show yourselves to the priests." As they were going they were cleansed. And one of them, realizing he had been healed, returned, glorifying God in a loud voice; and he fell at the feet of Jesus and thanked him. He was a Samaritan. Jesus said in reply, "Ten were cleansed, were they not? Where are the other nine? Has none but this foreigner returned to give thanks to God?" Then he said to him, "Stand up and go; your faith has saved you."

Reflecting on the Word

In biblical times, there was neither cure nor understanding of leprosy. Lepers were not welcomed anywhere, and they longed for relief. Of interest is that Jesus sent them away but did not touch or say words over them. The only leper who returned to express gratitude was the ultimate outcast: a leper and Samaritan. Who could have imagined this outcome? Jesus praised the Samaritan's expression of faith.

......ON THE WAY TO MASS:

I wonder how you feel when people ignore you? What if you were always sick and sad?

ON THE WAY HOME FROM MASS: ......

How can each person in our family work to include those who are on the margins or not welcome?

Living the Word

In the movie *Pollyanna*, a new girl in the town made up "the glad game" because she had no friends at first. Ask family members to share a list of things for which they are grateful. Nothing is off limits: friends, relatives, teachers, pets, food, experiences, and most importantly, faith. Save the lists, and review on the next rainy or "boring" day, and encourage some additions! Our journey of faith opens many opportunities for Christian gratitude.

October 16, 2016

Twenty-Ninth Sunday in Ordinary Time

Hearing the Word

Luke 18:1–8

In the name of the Father, and of the Son, and of the Holy Spirit.

Jesus told his disciples a parable about the necessity for them to pray always without becoming weary. He said, "There was a judge in a certain town who neither feared God nor respected any human being. And a widow in that town used to come to him and say, 'Render a just decision for me against my adversary.' For a long time the judge was unwilling, but eventually he thought, 'While it is true that I neither fear God nor respect any human being, because this widow keeps bothering me I shall deliver a just decision for her lest she finally come and strike me.'" The Lord said, "Pay attention to what the dishonest judge says. Will not God then secure the rights of his chosen ones who call out to him day and night? Will he be slow to answer them? I tell you, he will see to it that justice is done for them speedily. But when the Son of Man comes, will he find faith on earth?"

Reflecting on the Word

From the beginning of today's Gospel, we know that the point of the parable is that we should pray all of the time. In the story, the widow manages to wear down the dishonest judge, and he finally provides her with a decision. Jesus orders his disciples to pray and not tire. Prayer is one way that faith can deepen and become stronger. The challenge is to pray, so that God will find faith among us at the end of time.

...... ON THE WAY TO MASS:

I wonder why we hear many stories from Jesus about not becoming discouraged. What gives us hope?

ON THE WAY HOME FROM MASS: ......

Our weather is changing as fall descends. What good ideas about faith have we harvested since summer?

Living the Word

Search YouTube for musical settings of the Our Father. Spend some time listening and reflecting on different arrangements of a prayer that is known to all. Marvel at the number of musical arrangements of this prayer. Challenge and remind each family member to pray the Lord's Prayer at least twice a day this week. Guide preschoolers through the meaning of each phrase, and teach them the prayer, too. Pray unceasingly, as good disciples this week.

October 23, 2016

Thirtieth Sunday in Ordinary Time

Hearing the Word

Luke 18:9–14

In the name of the Father, and of the Son, and of the Holy Spirit.

Jesus addressed this parable to those who were convinced of their own righteousness and despised everyone else. "Two people went up to the temple area to pray; one was a Pharisee and the other was a tax collector. The Pharisee took up his position and spoke this prayer to himself, 'O God, I thank you that I am not like the rest of humanity — greedy, dishonest, adulterous — or even like this tax collector. I fast twice a week, and I pay tithes with my whole income.' But the tax collector stood off at a distance and would not even raise his eyes to heaven but beat his breast and prayed, 'O God, be merciful to me a sinner.' I tell you, the latter went home justified, not the former; for whoever exalts himself will be humbled, and the one who humbles himself will be exalted."

Reflecting on the Word

Although the Pharisee's prayer was true liturgical prayer, he trusted so completely in himself that he left God out of his life. His prayer began as thanksgiving but ended in praise of himself. The tax collector worked for the Romans and was despised by the Jews, but Jesus praised him because he knew his place before God. How we stand before God is important. In humility, we know that all we have comes from God. With such humility, our lives can praise God, and we can trust that God will be merciful to us.

......ON THE WAY TO MASS:

Sometimes we mistakenly think we're better than other people. How do you think God sees us every day?

ON THE WAY HOME FROM MASS: ......

I wonder if our family can be humble and still feel good about helping others. How could this happen?

Living the Word

Begin simply, and plan one family service evening every month. Thirty days can pass faster than you may think. Your family can do a simple task at the parish such as sweeping the church after the Saturday and Sunday Masses or taking out the trash. Keep your service low profile. Do something special on the way home, as a family, perhaps enjoying frozen yogurt or pizza with a coupon. Praise God for the opportunity to serve as unseen helpers.

October 30, 2016

Thirty-First Sunday in Ordinary Time

Hearing the Word

Luke 19:1–10

In the name of the Father, and of the Son, and of the Holy Spirit.

At that time, Jesus came to Jericho and intended to pass through the town. Now a man there named Zacchaeus, who was a chief tax collector and also a wealthy man, was seeking to see who Jesus was; but he could not see him because of the crowd, for he was short in stature. So he ran ahead and climbed a sycamore tree in order to see Jesus, who was about to pass that way. When he reached the place, Jesus looked up and said, "Zacchaeus, come down quickly, for today I must stay at your house." And he came down quickly and received him with joy. When they all saw this, they began to grumble, saying, "He has gone to stay at the house of a sinner." But Zacchaeus stood there and said to the Lord, "Behold, half of my possessions, Lord, I shall give to the poor, and if I have extorted anything from anyone I shall repay it four times over." And Jesus said to him, "Today salvation has come to this house because this man too is a descendant of Abraham. For the Son of Man has come to seek and to save what was lost."

Reflecting on the Word

Would anyone but fearful Zacchaeus climb a tree, just to check out Jesus? Jesus came to save the lost, and Zacchaeus was a tax collector, surely on the verge of being "lost." Although the crowd was probably amazed by Jesus' decision to stay with Zacchaeus, they had to see that Jesus was setting aside religious biases and social customs. Feeling righteous is not nearly as gratifying as taking a chance on becoming a real disciple. Zacchaeus' hospitality led to his salvation.

...... ON THE WAY TO MASS:

I wonder who might benefit if our family were a little more hospitable. How can we welcome people to come to church?

ON THE WAY HOME FROM MASS: ......

As the days shorten, the liturgical year is ending, too. How can we be light to others until Advent?

Living the Word

Make family time to re-create Zacchaeus' climb above the rooftops. If you have a two-story home, Zacchaeus can sit on the top step. Otherwise, use a step ladder in the living room for Zacchaeus. Pass out (pretzel) microphones, and give family members a chance to interview each other as the people on the ground. Ask the following: What is the tax collector doing? Who is Jesus and what did you hear him say? Is Jesus going to eat with Zacchaeus? Did Zacchaeus give you any clues to his motives?

November 1, 2016

Solemnity of All Saints

Hearing the Word

Matthew 5:3–12a

In the name of the Father, and of the Son, and of the Holy Spirit.

[Jesus said:] "Blessed are the poor in spirit, / for theirs is the Kingdom of heaven. / Blessed are they who mourn, / for they will be comforted. / Blessed are the meek, / for they will inherit the land. / Blessed are they who hunger and thirst for righteousness, / for they will be satisfied. / Blessed are the merciful, / for they will be shown mercy. / Blessed are the clean of heart, / for they will see God. / Blessed are the peacemakers, / for they will be called children of God. / Blessed are they who are persecuted for the sake of righteousness, / for theirs is the Kingdom of heaven. / Blessed are you when they insult you and persecute you and utter every kind of evil against you falsely because of me. / Rejoice and be glad, for your reward will be great in heaven."

Reflecting on the Word

The Beatitudes can be considered the commandments of the New Testament. Today we praise God for Jesus' Sermon on the Mount. Jesus provided so many ways for being good disciples, and we believe that those who have died and now live in God's presence are such disciples. Imagine a crowd so large, in the heavenly Kingdom, that we cannot see the end of the group. The reason that this group is countless is because our friends and relatives who have died are all there, people the world over and forever in time past.

......ON THE WAY TO MASS:

I wonder if we can really live the Beatitudes. Does Jesus want life to be happy and "blessed" for us?

ON THE WAY HOME FROM MASS: ......

Is happiness on earth just like happiness will be in heaven? How is heaven different?

Living the Word

Pray the Litany of the Saints, and make a special cake or special treat for the "saints to be." In an atmosphere of peace, ask the older children to finish the sentence, "When I get to heaven, it will be like . . . " The younger children can be the angels who welcome the new soul to heaven, saying, "I welcome you. You lived the Beatitudes." Make a cross for each person with the name of a favorite saint, and put it on the bedroom or refrigerator door. The crosses for the parents' will have the names of their children as their favorite saints.

November 6, 2016

Thirty-Second Sunday in Ordinary Time

Hearing the Word

Luke 20:27, 34–38

In the name of the Father, and of the Son, and of the Holy Spirit.

Some Sadducees, those who deny that there is a resurrection, came forward.

Jesus said to them, "The children of this age marry and remarry; but those who are deemed worthy to attain to the coming age and to the resurrection of the dead neither marry nor are given in marriage. They can no longer die, for they are like angels; and they are the children of God because they are the ones who will rise. That the dead will rise even Moses made known in the passage about the bush, when he called out 'Lord,' the God of Abraham, the God of Isaac, and the God of Jacob; and he is not God of the dead, but of the living, for to him all are alive."

Reflecting on the Word

During this part of Ordinary Time, the Old Testament links with the fulfillment that occurs in the New Testament, setting up a "back-to-the-future" scenario. There is still a covenant between God and man, and the relationship is not broken by death. We hear about the God of the living, and know that death is not the end of life. Resurrection continues life in another way. Jesus says that the life to come will not be as life is now. The Sadducees definitely don't understand the theology that Jesus speaks of.

...... ON THE WAY TO MASS:

We have God's promise of heaven if we live a faith-filled life. Whom do we know whose life is a model of faith?

ON THE WAY HOME FROM MASS: ......

The Sadducees were trying to trick Jesus. Have you ever been tricked away from following Jesus?

Living the Word

Pass markers and large pieces of paper cut in ovals. Have the younger children do a self-portrait "what I look like after my resurrection." The older children should mentor the artistic expressions, helping the younger ones imagine how "perfect" they will be. Nudge them to pay attention to hair, clothing, and facial expressions. Encourage creativity and maximize artistic imagination. Hang the drawings on a convenient wall and call it your Resurrection Gallery.

November 13, 2016

Thirty-Third Sunday in Ordinary Time

Hearing the Word

Luke 21:5–11

In the name of the Father, and of the Son, and of the Holy Spirit.

While some people were speaking about how the temple was adorned with costly stones and votive offerings, Jesus said, "All that you see here — the days will come when there will not be left a stone upon another stone that will not be thrown down."

Then they asked him, "Teacher, when will this happen? And what sign will there be when all these things are about to happen? He answered, "See that you not be deceived, for many will come in my name, saying, 'I am he,' and 'The time has come.' Do not follow them! When you hear of wars and insurrections, do not be terrified; for such things must happen first, but it will not immediately be the end." Then he said to them, "Nation will rise against nation, and kingdom against kingdom. There will be powerful earthquakes, famines, and plagues from place to place; and awesome sights and mighty signs will come from the sky."

Reflecting on the Word

Jesus speaks of the end of the world, and offers hope for those who persevere in faith. Many people have experienced some of the difficulties that Jesus said would happen, and these things happen while time passes. This Scripture points from this world (the destruction of the Temple, which was priceless to the Jews) to the next (not a historical moment, but a time of fulfillment). We still await the day when God will come in majesty and make everything right.

...... ON THE WAY TO MASS:

Should we be concerned about the end of time? Should our concerns be with how we pray and live?

ON THE WAY HOME FROM MASS: ......

The Gospel told about a huge, beautiful temple that took a hundred years to build. Can buildings last forever? What could last forever?

Living the Word

We just have one more Sunday in the liturgical year. The new liturgical year will begin in two weeks with the First Sunday of Advent. Talk about the calendar year being different from the Church's liturgical year. Decorate the calendar days for the next two weeks, making a colorful countdown. Mark a week from today as the Solemnity of Jesus Christ, King of the Universe, and talk about the kind of king that Jesus is for us. Do we really need a king? Begin to plan a simple celebration for November 27, which is the liturgical "new year's day."

November 20, 2016

Solemnity of Our Lord Jesus Christ, King of the Universe

Hearing the Word

Luke 23:35–43

In the name of the Father, and of the Son, and of the Holy Spirit.

The rulers sneered at Jesus and said, "He saved others, let him save himself if he is the chosen one, the Christ of God." Even the soldiers jeered at him. As they approached to offer him wine they called out, "If you are King of the Jews, save yourself." Above him there was an inscription that read, "This is the King of the Jews."

Now one of the criminals hanging there reviled Jesus, saying, "Are you not the Christ? Save yourself and us." The other, however, rebuking him, said in reply, "Have you no fear of God, for you are subject to the same condemnation? And indeed, we have been condemned justly, for the sentence we received corresponds to our crimes, but this man has done nothing criminal." Then he said, "Jesus, remember me when you come into your kingdom." He replied to him, "Amen, I say to you, today you will be with me in Paradise."

Reflecting on the Word

This Gospel reading recounts a story of mistaken identity. What the soldiers and the rulers saw was a criminal, and they challenged Jesus to save himself. But for Jesus to save himself from the Cross was not God's plan. It was God's plan that Jesus would die and gain admittance to the Kingdom for all of us, forevermore. The proof of redemption came from the so-called "good thief" who recognized, for an unknown reason, that Jesus was indeed the Son of God. A miracle realized, on the day of Crucifixion.

...... ON THE WAY TO MASS:

I wonder how different life would be if we had a real king, instead of a president?

ON THE WAY HOME FROM MASS: ......

Jesus was the king of our hearts, even on the Cross. Would you have believed his promise of paradise?

Living the Word

Break out the glitter and the faux jewels so the younger children can make at least one crown, for the centerpiece of the family living area. Have at least one conversation with the older children, reminding them that, even if they are tempted to make a bad decision, they can remember Jesus' Death on the Cross, and that he died for us. Making a good decision is the least we can do for Jesus, who paid the ultimate price for our redemption. Let the children know that we are always loved.

November 27, 2016

First Sunday of Advent

Hearing the Word

Matthew 24:37–42

In the name of the Father, and of the Son, and of the Holy Spirit.

Jesus said to his disciples: "As it was in the days of Noah, so it will be at the coming of the Son of Man. In those days before the flood, they were eating and drinking, marrying and giving in marriage, up to the day that Noah entered the ark. They did not know until the flood came and carried them all away. So will it be also at the coming of the Son of Man. Two men will be out in the field; one will be taken, and one will be left. Two women will be grinding at the mill; one will be taken, and one will be left. Therefore, stay awake! For you do not know on which day your Lord will come. Be sure of this: if the master of the house had known the hour of night when the thief was coming, he would have stayed awake and not let his house be broken into. So too, you also must be prepared, for at an hour you do not expect, the Son of Man will come."

Reflecting on the Word

We are told to stay awake and be prepared. But why should we be alert? We should be alert that we are living a good life. Many people prepare for Christmas by shopping for gifts. Matthew reminds us that Jesus was talking only with his disciples and giving them an idea of how to live. We anticipate joy in heaven. Jesus' idea isn't about staying awake and being sleep deprived, but rather paying attention to the danger of ignoring God. If our lives do not include preparation for a heavenly reward, then life is hopeless. Rejoice in the hope that we have.

...... ON THE WAY TO MASS:

I wonder if we'll see an Advent wreath in church today. Will the music be different during Advent?

ON THE WAY HOME FROM MASS: ......

I wonder how we can prepare simply and sacramentally for Christmas. What is most important to everyone about Christmas?

Living the Word

The four candles of Advent can be in a wreath or simply gathered together. It's the gradual lighting of each weekly candle that brings the season of Christmas a bit closer. Choose a special time each Sunday to light a new candle for Advent, and during the coming week pray, "Come, O Lord, and be the light in our lives." Use the wreath at breakfast, at dinner, or whenever two or three persons are gathered. Celebrate the Sacrament of Penance, then have a special Advent "rejoicing treat" on the way home.

December 4, 2016

Second Sunday of Advent

Hearing the Word

Matthew 3:1–6

In the name of the Father, and of the Son, and of the Holy Spirit

John the Baptist appeared, preaching in the desert of Judea and saying, "Repent, for the kingdom of heaven is at hand!" It was of him that the prophet Isaiah had spoken when he said: / *A voice of one crying out in the desert,* / *Prepare the way of the Lord,* / *make straight his paths.* / John wore clothing made of camel's hair and had a leather belt around his waist. His food was locusts and wild honey. At that time Jerusalem, all Judea, and the whole region around the Jordan were going out to him and were being baptized by him in the Jordan River as they acknowledged their sins.

Reflecting on the Word

John the Baptist said that people should repent and change their lives. He knew that some people wanted to be baptized just because it was popular, but he begged people to be sincere about turning back to God. John also reminded the people who came to spy on him that someone greater than he was coming. He just didn't say when this Savior would arrive. This Gospel story points out that we always need to prepare for the coming of Christ, even though we don't know when it will occur.

......ON THE WAY TO MASS:

Listen carefully to the Gospel and learn that John the Baptist was a wild-looking man. Why did he baptize so many people?

ON THE WAY HOME FROM MASS: ......

Everyone's baptismal day is as important as a birthday. Do you know what day and date you were baptized?

Living the Word

Make a chart that includes the baptismal date of each family member. Place a calendar for the coming year in a prominent place and post all of the baptismal dates. Discuss how to celebrate those days during the year. One way to celebrate is to let the baptismal day person pick one special thing to eat for supper (breakfast or lunch). You can always sing the birthday song with different words. Baptism gives everyone the perfect gift: a reward in heaven.

December 8, 2016

Solemnity of the Immaculate Conception of the Blessed Virgin Mary

Hearing the Word

Luke 1:26–30a, 35b–38a

In the name of the Father, and of the Son, and of the Holy Spirit.

The angel Gabriel was sent from God to a town of Galilee called Nazareth, to a virgin betrothed to a man named Joseph, of the house of David, and the virgin's name was Mary. And coming to her, he said, "Hail, full of grace! The Lord is with you." But she was greatly troubled at what was said and pondered what sort of greeting this might be. Then the angel said to her, "Do not be afraid, Mary, . . . the Holy Spirit will come upon you, and the power of the Most High will overshadow you. Therefore the child to be born will be called holy, the Son of God. And behold, Elizabeth, your relative, has also conceived a son in her old age, and this is the sixth month for her who was called barren; for nothing will be impossible for God." Mary said, "Behold, I am the handmaid of the Lord. May it be done to me according to your will." Then the angel departed from her.

Reflecting on the Word

Mary responded to the angel that she would fully cooperate with God's plan for her. Her "yes" required great trust and even greater faith. Mary believed the angel because she knew that nothing is impossible with God. Her love for God was such that she trusted the message that the angel brought. Mary was totally free from original sin, so that she could be Jesus' human mother.

......ON THE WAY TO MASS:

I wonder why it's so important to honor the Blessed Virgin Mary today by going to Mass?

ON THE WAY HOME FROM MASS:......

Mary was "full of grace," so she was able to accept the love of God and trust the message from the angel. Do you feel God's love, or grace, in your life?

Living the Word

Make (or buy) cookie dough, and use a cookie cutter with the letters "Y" "E" and "S." Decorate cutouts with colored sugar and talk about the ideas and actions that we should say "yes" to: helping others, listening with kindness, playing fair, doing small extra favors for people who need help. Talk about being a little more "yes" and much less "no" or "maybe" this Advent. What good habit could we say "yes" to, this Advent? Our yes is no different than Mary's, if we have faith when we say it.

December 11, 2016

Third Sunday of Advent

Hearing the Word

Matthew 11:2–6

In the name of the Father, and of the Son, and of the Holy Spirit.

When John the Baptist heard in prison of the works of the Christ, he sent his disciples to Jesus with this question, "Are you the one who is to come, or should we look for another?" Jesus said to them in reply, "Go and tell John what you hear and see: the blind regain their sight, the lame walk, lepers are cleansed, the deaf hear, the dead are raised, and the poor have the good news proclaimed to them. And blessed is the one who takes no offense at me."

Reflecting on the Word

People in power were afraid of John the Baptist, so he ended up in prison. When John sent his followers to ask Jesus if he was the Savior, Jesus pointed to the miracles that he had performed. Jesus praised John the Baptist and let people know that no one was as good a person as John. While Jesus affirmed that John was God's messenger, John learned that Jesus was the Messiah.

...... ON THE WAY TO MASS:

Advent is about joyful anticipation and especially about patience. What makes us impatient during Advent?

ON THE WAY HOME FROM MASS: ......

John the Baptist needed patience as he sat in prison. How can we be more patient with ourselves and others?

Living the Word

Encourage each family member to perform a random act of kindness for someone this week. Give each child a dollar and instruct them to patiently find a chance to make that dollar work to help another person. Let the younger ones know that even placing the dollar in Sunday's collection can make a difference. Perhaps the older children could buy a snack for a friend or put the dollar in the Salvation Army's red kettle. It takes patience to think of a kind act with a small amount of money.

December 18, 2016

Fourth Sunday of Advent

Hearing the Word

Matthew 1:18–24

In the name of the Father, and of the Son, and of the Holy Spirit.

This is how the birth of Jesus Christ came about. When his mother Mary was betrothed to Joseph, but before they lived together, she was found with child through the Holy Spirit. Joseph her husband, since he was a righteous man, yet unwilling to expose her to shame, decided to divorce her quietly. Such was his intention when, behold, the angel of the Lord appeared to him in a dream and said, "Joseph, son of David, do not be afraid to take Mary your wife into your home. For it is through the Holy Spirit that this child has been conceived in her. She will bear a son and you are to name him Jesus, because he will save his people from their sins." All this took place to fulfill what the Lord had said through the prophet: / *Behold, the virgin shall conceive and bear a son, / and they shall name him Emmanuel, /* which means "God is with us." When Joseph awoke, he did as the angel of the Lord had commanded him and took his wife into his home.

Reflecting on the Word

We learn in the Gospel about Mary's early pregnancy, and of Joseph's concerns. A Jewish woman stayed in her father's house until an appropriate lapse of time, because marriage was an economic transaction rather than about love. Joseph would take Mary into his home after about a year. Joseph is aware that he has not caused Mary to conceive, and he is distressed. It was with an enormous amount of trust in God that Joseph followed the will of God, once the angel appeared.

...... ON THE WAY TO MASS:

We hear today of Joseph's faith and trust. Would we be faith filled if God sent us a new baby at Christmas?

ON THE WAY HOME FROM MASS: ......

Our patience is nearly exhausted! What do we wait for this Christmas season? When will the rejoicing begin?

Living the Word

Put paper and pens beside an Idea Box. As you finish the decorations for Christmas, talk together about how Christmas can be a holy day/season, and also a holiday. Everyone has to put at least three ideas for a holy day in the suggestion box, sometime in the next three days. On day four, empty the box and make a list to be posted on the refrigerator. Invite the youngest or the oldest child to pick two ways that the family can make Christmas holy. Perhaps a new family Christmas tradition will come from these ideas.

December 25, 2016

Solemnity of the Nativity of the Lord

Hearing the Word

Luke 2:1, 3–7a, 8–14

In the name of the Father, and of the Son, and of the Holy Spirit.

In those days a decree went out from Caesar Augustus that the whole world should be enrolled. And Joseph too went up from Galilee from the town of Nazareth to Judea, to the city of David that is called Bethlehem, because he was of the house and family of David, to be enrolled with Mary, his betrothed, who was with child. While they were there, the time came for her to have her child, and she gave birth to her firstborn son.

Now there were shepherds in that region living in the fields and keeping the night watch over their flock. The angel of the Lord appeared to them and the glory of the Lord shone around them, and they were struck with great fear. The angel said to them, "Do not be afraid; for behold, I proclaim to you good news of great joy that will be for all the people. For today in the city of David a savior has been born for you who is Christ and Lord. And this will be a sign for you: you will find an infant wrapped in swaddling clothes and lying in a manger." And suddenly there was a multitude of the heavenly host with the angel, praising God and saying: / "Glory to God in the highest / and on earth peace to those on whom his favor rests."

Reflecting on the Word

This Midnight Mass Gospel reading opens the season of Christmas. God kept his promise and sent a Savior into the world, and the glory of God couldn't have been any brighter and more glorious, according to St. Luke. We learn that Jesus was born in Bethlehem, and that he was born into a poor family. This Gospel reminds us, tenderly, that we have the same hope and the same promise that the angels celebrated. We have a new relationship with a loving God through this intimate birth of a tiny boy.

...... ON THE WAY TO MASS:

I hope everyone listens to tonight's Gospel. How can we show our joy and gratitude for Jesus' birth?

ON THE WAY HOME FROM MASS: ......

Did anyone notice that Jesus wasn't born in his hometown and there were no friends to welcome him?

Living the Word

This Christmas, invite someone to be a guest in your home for a meal, a movie, or even a snack and conversation. It could be a new family from your workplace or in the parish. It could even be an older person who would be alone during the season of Christmas. Welcome the stranger, remembering that the angels were the only ministers of hospitality when the Son of God was born to Mary and Joseph. Make the Christmas Gospel real to another family, with hospitality from yours.

January 1, 2017

SOLEMNITY OF MARY, THE HOLY MOTHER OF GOD

Hearing the Word

Luke 2:16–21

In the name of the Father, and of the Son, and of the Holy Spirit.

The shepherds went in haste to Bethlehem and found Mary and Joseph, and the infant lying in the manger. When they saw this, they made known the message that had been told them about this child. All who heard it were amazed by what had been told them by the shepherds. And Mary kept all these things, reflecting on them in her heart. Then the shepherds returned, glorifying and praising God for all they had heard and seen, just as it had been told to them.

When eight days were completed for his circumcision, he was named Jesus, the name given him by the angel before he was conceived in the womb.

Reflecting on the Word

The Gospel reflects Mary as a mother who stores memories and Joseph as learning what the angels had announced to the shepherds. We learn of Jesus' circumcision according to the Jewish law, and his naming, which was foretold to Mary at the Annunciation. Although the focus of the Scripture is Mary, other themes emerge. There is a perception of peace and of Mary's faith. Added to this were the tender shepherds whose visit alerted Mary and Joseph to the truth of the eventual kingship of this newborn.

...... ON THE WAY TO MASS:

As we begin a new calendar year, what can our family do that begins anew how we practice our faith?

ON THE WAY HOME FROM MASS: ......

I wonder if we can journey toward wholeness as a family in 2017. Can we move from petty discord to peace?

Living the Word

Remember that the Christmas season isn't over yet. Bring branches inside and force some colorful growth, adding an unexpected burst of color that outlasts the poinsettias. Help the children to create a simple "magi crèche," homemade from scraps of fabric, gift wrap, and old jewelry, to emphasize the continuation of the season. The blessing of the home this week, the playing of carols, and perhaps clouds of incense drifting outdoors are activities that remind us still of Christmas.

January 8, 2017

Solemnity of the Epiphany of the Lord

Hearing the Word

Matthew 2:1–4, 7–11

In the name of the Father, and of the Son, and of the Holy Spirit.

When Jesus was born in Bethlehem of Judea, in the days of King Herod, behold, magi from the east arrived in Jerusalem, saying, "Where is the newborn king of the Jews? We saw his star at its rising and have come to do him homage." When King Herod heard this, he was greatly troubled, and all Jerusalem with him. Assembling all the chief priests and the scribes of the people, he inquired of them where the Christ was to be born. Then Herod called the magi secretly and ascertained from them the time of the star's appearance. He sent them to Bethlehem and said, "Go and search diligently for the child. When you have found him, bring me word, that I too may go and do him homage." After their audience with the king they set out. And behold, the star that they had seen at its rising preceded them, until it came and stopped over the place where the child was. They were overjoyed at seeing the star, and on entering the house they saw the child with Mary his mother. They prostrated themselves and did him homage. Then they opened their treasures and offered him gifts of gold, frankincense, and myrrh.

Reflecting on the Word

This wondrous Scripture appears almost as a drama, with Herod making a great effort to find the new ruler who would shepherd Israel, using the Magi as informants. The text names three gifts, but doesn't name how many Magi there were. In its clarity and simplicity, the Gospel tells us that Jesus came not just for the Jews but for foreigners from many lands.

...... ON THE WAY TO MASS:

The Gospel says that the Magi followed a star. How can we find Jesus today, if there is no star to lead us?

ON THE WAY HOME FROM MASS: ......

I wonder what we can do to light the way for Jesus to come into school, work, and family activities?

Living the Word

This week, celebrate the star that led the Magi to Jesus! Drape inexpensive lights in a family area, apart from the Christmas tree. As a family, make star cookies, eat star-shaped sandwiches, and write a new year's resolution—just one—on a star. Encourage all family members to keep the star in a secret place until Ash Wednesday. On that day, everyone should take out their stars and check to see if they spread the light of Christ with the resolution, or if it needs to be renewed during Lent. Each resolution lights the way to living more like Jesus.

January 15, 2017

Second Sunday in Ordinary Time

Hearing the Word

John 1:29–34

In the name of the Father, and of the Son, and of the Holy Spirit.

John the Baptist saw Jesus coming toward him and said, “Behold, the Lamb of God, who takes away the sin of the world. He is the one of whom I said, ‘A man is coming after me who ranks ahead of me because he existed before me.’ I did not know him, but the reason why I came baptizing with water was that he might be made known to Israel.” John testified further, saying, “I saw the Spirit come down like a dove from heaven and remain upon him. I did not know him, but the one who sent me to baptize with water told me, ‘On whomever you see the Spirit come down and remain, he is the one who will baptize with the Holy Spirit.’ Now I have seen and testified that he is the Son of God.”

Reflecting on the Word

John the Baptist connected his experience of the Spirit hovering over Jesus with his mission to serve as a baptizer. He was rewarded with the certainty that Jesus was indeed the one "who will baptize with the Holy Spirit." Fearless John the Baptist! As wily and rough as he was depicted to be, he made known a beautiful, gentle truth: Jesus as the Son of God was announced by John to Israel.

......ON THE WAY TO MASS:

Someone asks, "Whose disciple are you?" How would you respond to this question?

ON THE WAY HOME FROM MASS: ......

I wonder whether we would believe John the Baptist if he introduced Jesus today. Who announces Jesus today?

Living the Word

Jesus didn't really need to be baptized, but it happened so that he could follow religious history. He also let John publicly introduce him to Israel. Attend a Baptism at your parish or a nearby parish; Baptisms are often celebrated during Mass on a weekend. Help the children reflect by asking afterwards: What did you see or hear during that Baptism that announced publicly that the child was now a member of a new family of faith? Was there ever a moment in your life when you felt without a doubt that God loved you?

January 22, 2017

Third Sunday in Ordinary Time

Hearing the Word

Matthew 4:12–17

In the name of the Father, and of the Son, and of the Holy Spirit.

When Jesus heard that John had been arrested, he withdrew to Galilee. He left Nazareth and went to live in Capernaum by the sea, in the region of Zebulun and Naphtali, that what had been said through Isaiah the prophet might be fulfilled: / *Land of Zebulun and land of Naphtali, / the way to the sea, beyond the Jordan, / Galilee of the Gentiles, / the people who sit in darkness have seen a great light, / on those dwelling in a land overshadowed by death / light has arisen.* / From that time on, Jesus began to preach and say, "Repent, for the kingdom of heaven is at hand."

Reflecting on the Word

Although John's imprisonment coincided with the beginning of Jesus' public life, Jesus didn't leave Nazareth to avoid the implications of John's arrest. The New Age had finally arrived. The image of Jesus as the "great light" that Isaiah spoke of is clear. Equally obvious is the mission of Jesus to preach repentance and anticipate the Kingdom of God for those who would become disciples. Jesus came to proclaim the Good News, the news that this Kingdom was at hand. How radical was Jesus' notion!

...... ON THE WAY TO MASS:

I wonder how you know if God calls you to the priesthood or to become a sister or brother. How do you hear God?

ON THE WAY HOME FROM MASS: ......

I wonder what you would do if Jesus phoned you to be a disciple. How would you respond to his call?

Living the Word

Ordinary Time isn't really "ordinary." It comes from the word *ordinal* and is the way we count the weeks of the liturgical year that are outside of the seasons of Advent, Christmas, Lent, and Easter. The beginning of Ordinary Time is generally during the winter throughout the United States. Anticipate the Feast of the Presentation of the Lord (Candlemas) on February 2 by collecting candles for your table. Call the "family of disciples" together for a reading of Psalm 27 (A and B) several times during this week, even as mealtime or bedtime prayer. God lights the way for disciples!

January 29, 2017

Fourth Sunday in Ordinary Time

Hearing the Word

Matthew 5:1–12a

In the name of the Father, and of the Son, and of the Holy Spirit.

When Jesus saw the crowds, he went up the mountain, and after he had sat down, his disciples came to him. He began to teach them, saying: / "Blessed are the poor in spirit, / for theirs is the kingdom of heaven. / Blessed are they who mourn, / for they will be comforted. / Blessed are the meek, / for they will inherit the land. / Blessed are they who hunger and thirst for righteousness, / for they will be satisfied. / Blessed are the merciful, / for they will be shown mercy. / Blessed are the clean of heart, / for they will see God. / Blessed are the peacemakers, / for they will be called children of God. / Blessed are they who are persecuted for the sake of righteousness, / for theirs is the kingdom of heaven. / Blessed are you when they insult you and persecute you and utter every kind of evil against you falsely because of me. Rejoice and be glad, for your reward will be great in heaven."

Reflecting on the Word

In giving the disciples the Beatitudes, Jesus is showing them a new way of living. These teachings have set the standard of what a Christian should do to enter heaven. Living these nine Beatitudes could not have fallen easily on Jesus' listeners, but were held out as a model of life. We understand the word "blessed" as "you will be blessed," indicating grace in the future rather than a consequence for the present time.

......ON THE WAY TO MASS:

I wonder how our family can learn more about being disciples. What would Pope Francis say to us about this?

ON THE WAY HOME FROM MASS: ......

If Jesus had a blog for disciples today, what would he write?

Living the Word

Play a calming instrumental CD and invite the children to put on a pretend "religious imagination hat." Set a timer and give the children eight minutes to think of one or two new beatitudes. Think: Blessed are the thoughtful, for they will be God's best friends in heaven, or Blessed are those who are sick, because they will have perfect health in heaven. Applaud each new beatitude and recognize the shared wisdom about discipleship.

February 5, 2017

Fifth Sunday in Ordinary Time

Hearing the Word

Matthew 5:13–16

In the name of the Father, and of the Son, and of the Holy Spirit.

Jesus said to his disciples: "You are the salt of the earth. But if salt loses its taste, with what can it be seasoned? It is no longer good for anything but to be thrown out and trampled underfoot. You are the light of the world. A city set on a mountain cannot be hidden. Nor do they light a lamp and then put it under a bushel basket; it is set on a lampstand, where it gives light to all in the house. Just so, your light must shine before others, that they may see your good deeds and glorify your heavenly Father."

Reflecting on the Word

Through the use of metaphors, Jesus continues to teach his closest followers. If salt loses its taste, it can't be good for seasoning; if disciples are not worthy followers of Jesus, they can't influence other followers. Considering Jesus' metaphor of being "light," the disciples were being told that they should shine forth as examples in the way that they live and how they treat other people. Jesus' teaching must have challenged his disciples.

...... ON THE WAY TO MASS:

Who was the greatest teacher that you have ever known? What did you learn from this teacher?

ON THE WAY HOME FROM MASS: ......

Jesus' disciples were ordinary people. Can you name an ordinary person who is a good disciple of Jesus?

Living the Word

Share two songs that have an instructive text about what it's like to be a follower of Jesus: "They'll Know We Are Christians" (Peter Scholtes, 1966, © St. Brendan's) and "We Are the Light of the World" (Jean A. Grief, © 1966). Teach the refrains first, and prompt the older children who are better readers to sing or say the verses. Both of these songs contain wisdom that emphasizes Matthew's Gospel this week. Encourage the children to think of hand gestures for the songs.

February 12, 2017

Sixth Sunday in Ordinary Time

Hearing the Word

Matthew 5:20–22a, 27–28, 33–34a, 37

In the name of the Father, and of the Son, and of the Holy Spirit.

[Jesus said to his disciples:] "I tell you, unless your righteousness surpasses that of the scribes and Pharisees, you will not enter the kingdom of heaven.

"You have heard that it was said to your ancestors, *You shall not kill; and whoever kills will be liable to judgment.* But I say to you, whoever is angry with his brother will be liable to judgment.

"You have heard that it was said, *You shall not commit adultery*. But I say to you, everyone who looks at a woman with lust has already committed adultery with her in his heart.

"Again, you have heard that it was said to your ancestors, *Do not take a false oath, but make good to the Lord all that you vow*. But I say to you, do not swear at all. Let your 'Yes' mean 'Yes,' and your 'No' mean 'No.' Anything more is from the evil one."

Reflecting on the Word

In Matthew's account of the Gospel, Jesus continues to teach his closest disciples about the mysteries of the Kingdom of Heaven and about making the right choices. When Jesus says, "Amen," he emphasizes that what he says is the truth, and "I say to you" means that he is the authority on the teaching. As he teaches the disciples, Jesus is taking the old law and reimagining it in the new order. Clearly, the disciples are hearing radically new teaching from the Master.

......ON THE WAY TO MASS:

The Catholic Church has a catechism, published in many languages. How do we use a catechism? (Hint: to teach about our faith.)

ON THE WAY HOME FROM MASS: ......

Jesus is teaching his disciples about good behavior. Did the disciples need religious education?

Living the Word

The Gospel according to Matthew is addressed to people who have already experienced the Good News of Jesus. Beginning today, make each day this week a "Good News day." Every family member should have one piece of good news ready; pick a different person each day, and ask, "What's your Good News?" The individual should identify something good he or she has been done as well as explain why the act was a good thing to do. Something kind that was done to/for them also could be shared. Sharing individual experiences can shape our good behaviors.

February 19, 2017

Seventh Sunday in Ordinary Time

Hearing the Word

Matthew 5:38–48

In the name of the Father, and of the Son, and of the Holy Spirit.

Jesus said to his disciples, "You have heard that it was said, *An eye for an eye and a tooth for a tooth*. But I say to you, offer no resistance to the one who is evil. When someone strikes you on your right cheek, turn the other one as well. If anyone wants to go to law with you over your tunic, hand over your cloak as well. Should anyone press you into service for one mile, go for two miles. Give to the one who asks of you, and do not turn your back on one who wants to borrow.

"You have heard that it was said, *You shall love your neighbor and hate your enemy*. But I say to you, love your enemies and pray for those who persecute you, that you may be children of your heavenly Father, for he makes his sun rise on the bad and the good, and causes rain to fall on the just and the unjust. For if you love those who love you, what recompense will you have? Do not the tax collectors do the same? And if you greet your brothers only, what is unusual about that? Do not the pagans do the same? So be perfect, just as your heavenly Father is perfect."

Reflecting on the Word

Jesus teaches us how to be holy. The examples Jesus uses may seem exaggerated, yet we know that true goodness is a challenge. Jesus is reinterpreting the Mosaic law when he speaks of nonviolence and loving others despite rejection. We can see that being a follower of Jesus isn't easy, and sometimes we will need to ask God for help. Being "perfect" means that being like God is a goal for our lives.

...... ON THE WAY TO MASS:

I wonder if we will get new ideas after hearing today's Gospel. What does "turning the other cheek" mean?

ON THE WAY HOME FROM MASS: ......

God is holy, so we need to be more like God. How can we be more like Jesus, here on earth?

Living the Word

Put forth a challenge to family members to make an effort to love "an enemy." Ask them to write the name of a person with whom they struggle at work, school, day care, or the playground, perhaps even at home. Give everyone an envelope to put their name on and seal another name inside. Put the envelopes in a box labeled, "Be Like Jesus." Before next Sunday, pass the envelopes around to their owners; ask each person to open their envelope and to discard it if they have tried to be more Christlike. Tape the envelope closed again if another week's effort is needed.

February 26, 2017

Eighth Sunday in Ordinary Time

Hearing the Word

Matthew 6:24–33

In the name of the Father, and of the Son, and of the Holy Spirit.

Jesus said to his disciples, "No one can serve two masters. He will either hate one and love the other, or be devoted to one and despise the other. You cannot serve God and mammon.

"Therefore, I tell you, do not worry about your life, what you will eat or drink, or about your body, what you will wear. Is not life more than food and the body more than clothing? Look at the birds in the sky; they do not sow or reap, they gather nothing into barns, yet your heavenly Father feeds them. Are not you more important than they? Can any of you by worrying add a single moment to your life-span? Why are you anxious about clothes? Learn from the way the wild flowers grow. They do not work or spin. But I tell you that not even Solomon in all his splendor was clothed like one of them. If God so clothes the grass of the field, which grows today and is thrown into the oven tomorrow, will he not much more provide for you, O you of little faith? So do not worry and say, 'What are we to eat?' or 'What are we to drink?' or 'What are we to wear?' All these things the pagans seek. Your heavenly Father knows that you need them all. But seek first the kingdom of God and his righteousness, and all these things will be given you besides."

Reflecting on the Word

It's difficult to hear "do not worry" in the United States in the twenty-first century. This teaching of Jesus sounds just as radical to us today as it must have to the disciples of the first century. But we can be loyal to God, and we can trust in God. Wealth is something that can distract us from loving God. But many habits can distract too. Jesus challenges the disciples and us to have confidence in the love and care of God.

...... ON THE WAY TO MASS:

God gave each of us special gifts and talents. Do we get overwhelmed, worrying about being successful?

ON THE WAY HOME FROM MASS: ......

What things in life get in the way of serving others, and being more like Jesus in the way we act?

Living the Word

Lent begins in a week. Round up the palms from last year, and return them to the parish for ashes. Share a teachable moment about where those Lenten ashes come from. Challenge everyone to "give" rather than "give up" this Lent. Giving and serving can create a new habit. Ask family members: What can you do that is a positive step to being holier? What bad habit can you replace with a good habit? Plan a day each week when you will eat supper more simply, serving rice and beans or soup and bread.

March 5, 2017

First Sunday of Lent

Hearing the Word

Matthew 4:1–11

In the name of the Father, and of the Son, and of the Holy Spirit.

At that time Jesus was led by the Spirit into the desert to be tempted by the devil. He fasted for forty days and forty nights, and afterwards he was hungry. The tempter approached and said to him, "If you are the Son of God, command that these stones become loaves of bread." He said in reply, "It is written: / *One does not live on bread alone, / but on every word that comes forth / from the mouth of God.*"

Then the devil took him to the holy city, and made him stand on the parapet of the temple, and said to him, "If you are the Son of God, throw yourself down. For it is written: / *He will command his angels concerning you / and with their hands they will support you, / lest you dash your foot against a stone.*" Jesus answered him, "Again it is written, / *You shall not put the Lord, your God, to the test.*" / Then the devil took him up to a very high mountain, and showed him all the kingdoms of the world in their magnificence, and he said to him, "All these I shall give to you, if you will prostrate yourself and worship me." At this, Jesus said to him, "Get away, Satan! It is written: / *The Lord, your God, shall you worship / and him alone shall you serve.*" Then the devil left him and, behold, angels came and ministered to him.

Reflecting on the Word

Today's Gospel shows that, in his humanity, Jesus was subject to temptation just as we are. We encounter temptation every day, and Jesus showed us that strength to get through tempting moments is possible from God. How could we ever doubt the goodness of God when we read this account? Although we can only imagine how "angels came and ministered" to Jesus, we should remember that God's love will calm our raging inclinations. Lent reminds us to ask for God's support to overcome temptation.

...... ON THE WAY TO MASS:

The Old Testament desert was thought to be a place of evil spirits. Is there a place of temptation for you?

ON THE WAY HOME FROM MASS: ......

Did you think of things to "just say 'no' to"? Now think of what you will say "yes" to this Lent.

Living the Word

Discuss as a family how we are called to love those we have a hard time loving. Each family member could decide to share Jesus' love with someone who isn't easy for him or her to love. Explain that conversion comes during times when it is difficult to love but we do so anyway. If we ask God to help us be better persons, we will get the aid we need. This is called grace. Find a small cross for each family member and tape it gently to the bathroom mirror or over the bed—find a place where we will be reminded that we carry a "little cross" during Lent.

March 12, 2017

Second Sunday of Lent

Hearing the Word

Matthew 17:1–9

In the name of the Father, and of the Son, and of the Holy Spirit.

Jesus took Peter, James, and John his brother, and led them up a high mountain by themselves. And he was transfigured before them; his face shone like the sun and his clothes became white as light. And behold, Moses and Elijah appeared to them, conversing with him. Then Peter said to Jesus in reply, "Lord, it is good that we are here. If you wish, I will make three tents here, one for you, one for Moses, and one for Elijah." While he was still speaking, behold, a bright cloud cast a shadow over them, then from the cloud came a voice that said, "This is my beloved Son, with whom I am well pleased; listen to him." When the disciples heard this, they fell prostrate and were very much afraid. But Jesus came and touched them, saying, "Rise, and do not be afraid." And when the disciples raised their eyes, they saw no one else but Jesus alone.

As they were coming down from the mountain, Jesus charged them, "Do not tell the vision to anyone until the Son of Man has been raised from the dead."

Reflecting on the Word

God is revealed to three disciples in today's Scripture, in a glorious miracle that was both frightening and enlightening as the disciples heard, "This is my beloved Son . . . listen to him." Once they recovered from the shock, Peter, James, and John must have felt emboldened for ministry. Even though they were not to share this experience yet, they were changed. We see the graciousness of God in revealing his Son Jesus to us. We know that God awaits us because the Son of Man truly has been raised from the dead.

...... ON THE WAY TO MASS:

This Lent, I want to become a better person. How and where can I find grace to help me?

ON THE WAY HOME FROM MASS: ......

Today's Gospel would make a great movie. What special effects would you use for the Transfiguration?

Living the Word

Set aside five extra minutes each day to pray together, ending the prayer with the question "What are you doing for Easter?" This doesn't necessarily need a verbal response, only a reminder from the prayer leader that Lent isn't about "giving up" but more importantly about making a change to be a good disciple of Jesus. The Litany of the Saints is a perfect prayer for this week, noting especially the Solemnity of St. Joseph, Spouse of the Blessed Virgin, ordinarily celebrated on March 19 and this year on March 20.

March 19, 2017

Third Sunday of Lent

Hearing the Word

John 4:6–7, 9 –11, 13–15, 23–26, 39a

In the name of the Father, and of the Son, and of the Holy Spirit.

Jesus, tired from his journey, sat down there at the well. It was about noon.

A woman of Samaria came to draw water. Jesus said to her, "Give me a drink." The Samaritan woman said to him, "How can you, a Jew, ask me, a Samaritan woman, for a drink?" . . . Jesus answered and said to her, "If you knew the gift of God and who is saying to you, 'Give me a drink,' you would have asked him and he would have given you living water." The woman said to him, "Sir, you do not even have a bucket and the cistern is deep; where then can you get this living water?" Jesus answered and said to her, "Everyone who drinks this water will be thirsty again; but whoever drinks the water I shall give will never thirst; the water I shall give will become in him a spring of water welling up to eternal life." The woman said to him, "Sir, give me this water, so that I may not be thirsty or have to keep coming here to draw water."

Jesus said to her, ". . . The hour is coming, and is now here, when true worshipers will worship the Father in Spirit and truth; and indeed the Father seeks such people to worship him. God is Spirit, and those who worship him must worship in Spirit and truth." The woman said to him, "I know that the Messiah is coming, the one called the

Christ; when he comes, he will tell us everything." Jesus said to her, "I am he, the one who is speaking with you."

Many of the Samaritans of that town began to believe in him because of the word of the woman who testified.

Reflecting on the Word

As the Samaritan woman began to understand the living water, she saw Jesus differently. Jesus pulls the woman into a deepening spirituality and to faith. She becomes a herald of the Savior.

......ON THE WAY TO MASS:

When are we thirsty for water? When do we thirst for things?

ON THE WAY HOME FROM MASS: ......

If we do something good, we feel happy or at peace. This takes grace. Shouldn't we "thirst" for grace?

Living the Word

Invite the family to use poster paper to make the chart, "On the Road to Easter." Cutouts, symbols, or name cards can be used for the people in the Gospel. Include Jesus, Peter, James, John, the Samaritan woman, and the transfigured Jesus. The road should be winding and include mountains (Sermon on the Mount and the mount of the Transfiguration). The beginning of the road should be marked and decorated as Lent, and the road should grow wider and wider until it reaches Easter. Later, have family members add the blind man, Lazarus, Martha and Mary, and Pharisees.

March 26, 2017

Fourth Sunday of Lent

Hearing the Word

John 9:1–3, 5–7

In the name of the Father, and of the Son, and of the Holy Spirit.

As Jesus passed by he saw a man blind from birth. His disciples asked him, "Rabbi, who sinned, this man or his parents that he was born blind?" Jesus answered, "Neither he nor his parents sinned; it is so the works of God may be visible through him." When he had said this, he spat on the ground and made clay with the saliva, and smeared the clay on his eyes, and said to him, "Go wash in the Pool of Siloam"—which means Sent—. So he went and washed, and came back able to see.

Reflecting on the Word

Jesus reveals himself again, this time to the blind man who was cured. All that was needed was an expression of faith. Without faith, the Pharisees did not recognize Jesus. Blind to Jesus, they lived in darkness. Jesus gave sight as the light of faith dawned on the man born blind. In biblical Israel, the sporadic movement of water at the pool at Siloam was thought to be curative. Jesus' public ministry continues to provide credible evidence that he was the one sent by the Father.

......ON THE WAY TO MASS:

Sometimes we are blind to seeing that Jesus loved us and died for our sins. How can we "see" Jesus today?

ON THE WAY HOME FROM MASS:......

Sometimes we are "blind" to growing in our faith. How do we lose our blindness to the love of God?

Living the Word

Plan an activity with 3-D glasses. Each family member puts on the glasses and eats a bowl of cereal (or soup) and tries to concentrate on not spilling anything. Does the food taste the same while wearing the glasses? Remove the glasses and allow the light to clear your vision. Talk about how to let the light of Jesus' love into your life. Isn't it better to live in the light of love, rather than the cloudy, distorted vision that you had with the 3-D glasses? Jesus, be light for our eyes!

April 2, 2017

Fifth Sunday of Lent

Hearing the Word

John 11:3–4, 20–27, 34–39, 41–43

In the name of the Father, and of the Son, and of the Holy Spirit.

The sisters of Lazarus sent word to Jesus, saying, "Master, the one you love is ill." When Jesus heard this he said, "This illness is not to end in death, but is for the glory of God, that the Son of God may be glorified through it."

When Martha heard that Jesus was coming, she went to meet him; but Mary sat at home. Martha said to Jesus, "Lord, if you had been here, my brother would not have died. But even now I know that whatever you ask of God, God will give you." Jesus said to her, "Your brother will rise." Martha said, "I know he will rise, in the resurrection on the last day." Jesus told her, "I am the resurrection and the life; whoever believes in me, even if he dies, will live, and everyone who lives and believes in me will never die. Do you believe this?" She said to him, "Yes, Lord. I have come to believe that you are the Christ, the Son of God, the one who is coming into the world."

He . . . said, "Where have you laid him?" They said to him, "Sir, come and see." And Jesus wept. So the Jews said, "See how he loved him." But some of them said, "Could not the one who opened the eyes of the blind man have done something so that this man would not have died?"

So Jesus . . . came to the tomb. It was a cave, and a stone lay across it. Jesus said, "Take away the stone." . . . So they took away the stone. And Jesus raised his eyes and said, "Father, I thank you for hearing me. I know that you always hear me; but because of the crowd here I have said this, that they may believe that you sent me." And when he had said this, he cried out in a loud voice, "Lazarus, come out!"

Reflecting on the Word

We experience the miracle today of Jesus raising his friend Lazarus from the dead. We learn of Martha's faith, and how Jesus waited to make sure that Lazarus was dead before he appeared on the scene. Life and death are woven throughout this passage of Lazarus' being called forth alive from the tomb. This life, death, and resurrection story parallels what is yet to come in Jesus' public life.

...... ON THE WAY TO MASS:

Jesus' power came directly from God. Do you see God's power in miracles today?

ON THE WAY HOME FROM MASS: ......

How was Jesus compassionate to Mary, Martha, and Lazarus? How did he show mercy?

Living the Word

Soon, we will celebrate Holy Week, which leads to Easter. The people we call "the elect" have been waiting to receive the sacraments of Baptism, Confirmation, and Eucharist. Make a joyful card of hope for each person or family awaiting the sacraments at the Easter Vigil. Pray an Our Father each day this week for the elect.

April 9, 2017

Palm Sunday of the Passion of the Lord

Hearing the Word

Matthew 21:1–11

In the name of the Father, and of the Son, and of the Holy Spirit.

When Jesus and the disciples drew near Jerusalem and came to Bethphage on the Mount of Olives, Jesus sent two disciples, saying to them, "Go into the village opposite you, and immediately you will find an ass tethered, and a colt with her. Untie them and bring them here to me. And if anyone should say anything to you, reply, 'The master has need of them.' Then he will send them at once." This happened so that what had been spoken through the prophet might be fulfilled: / *Say to daughter Zion, / "Behold, your king comes to you, / meek and riding on an ass, / and on a colt, the foal of a beast of burden."* / The disciples went and did as Jesus had ordered them. They brought the ass and the colt and laid their cloaks over them, and he sat upon them. The very large crowd spread their cloaks on the road, while others cut branches from the trees and strewed them on the road. The crowds preceding him and those following kept crying out and saying: / "Hosanna to the Son of David; / blessed is he who comes in the name of the Lord; / hosanna in the highest." / And when he entered Jerusalem the whole city was shaken and asked, "Who is this?" And the crowds replied, "This is Jesus the prophet, from Nazareth in Galilee."

Reflecting on the Word

There is evidence that, in fourth-century Jerusalem, a procession and liturgy inaugurated "the Great Week." Matthew's account is a collection of events in Jerusalem. Jesus has returned to face death. What could an account of these holy, yet awful, events contribute to faith? Amid beginning gladness, terrible tragedy looms. We have arrived full circle at the end of Jesus' public life and ministry. We know that our resurrection is guaranteed. We observe Passion Sunday with a glimpse of Easter joy.

...... ON THE WAY TO MASS:

I wonder if the family will absorb the Gospel today. Should we sit nearer the front of the church to hear better?

ON THE WAY HOME FROM MASS: ......

In the Gospel read at the procession, Jesus was welcomed as a king. What kind of king was Jesus?

Living the Word

Since Jesus' public ministry had convinced many that he would free them from Roman oppression, there must have been excitement in Jerusalem when the people heard Jesus was coming. Those people were misguided, and their joy quickly went away. Create and observe some time for peace and quiet today, possibly a family "holy (half?) hour" with no electronic distraction. Begin the time by praying the Apostles' Creed, and then allow each person to choose a quiet activity. In closing, mention that Lent ends soon.

April 16, 2017

Easter Sunday of the Resurrection of the Lord

Hearing the Word

John 20:1–9

In the name of the Father, and of the Son, and of the Holy Spirit.

On the first day of the week, Mary of Magdala came to the tomb early in the morning, while it was still dark, and saw the stone removed from the tomb. So she ran and went to Simon Peter and to the other disciple whom Jesus loved, and told them, "They have taken the Lord from the tomb, and we don't know where they put him." So Peter and the other disciple went out and came to the tomb. They both ran, but the other disciple ran faster than Peter and arrived at the tomb first; he bent down and saw the burial cloths there, but did not go in. When Simon Peter arrived after him, he went into the tomb and saw the burial cloths there, and the cloth that had covered his head, not with the burial cloths but rolled up in a separate place. Then the other disciple also went in, the one who had arrived at the tomb first, and he saw and believed. For they did not yet understand the Scripture that he had to rise from the dead.

Reflecting on the Word

The story begins in darkness, which seems symbolic as the realization of the empty tomb dawns on Mary of Magdala, running to get two disciples. It is probably light by the time she arrives back. Brave Simon Peter entered the empty tomb, but the first disciple ahead of him is the one who believed, upon seeing the burial cloths. There is indeed a glimpse of new life in this account, but even richer is the truth that the stone is rolled back and that Resurrection has triumphed over death.

......ON THE WAY TO MASS:

Many people will come to Mass today. How can we welcome the visitors and guests on this Easter Sunday?

ON THE WAY HOME FROM MASS:......

The Alleluia has returned! How many things can we think of, to be joyful about this Easter?

Living the Word

If individuals were baptized at your parish at the Easter Vigil, tell your children how these new members were welcomed into the Church through a service of song, story, and symbol. An Easter fire was lit, the congregation again sang the Alleluia, and the church was adorned with lilies. As a family, join your Easter joy to that of these new Christians as you eat special foods and wear your best clothes to Mass. Say "Alleluia" instead of hi or hello today, to everyone you meet. Take time to mark a new calendar, showing fifty days of unbelievable joy.

April 23, 2017

SECOND SUNDAY OF EASTER/ SUNDAY OF DIVINE MERCY

Hearing the Word

John 20:19, 24–29

In the name of the Father, and of the Son, and of the Holy Spirit.

On the evening of that first day of the week, when the doors were locked, where the disciples were, for fear of the Jews, Jesus came and stood in their midst and said to them, "Peace be with you."

Thomas, called Didymus, one of the Twelve, was not with them when Jesus came. So the other disciples said to him, "We have seen the Lord." But he said to them, "Unless I see the mark of the nails in his hands and put my finger into the nail marks and put my hand into his side, I will not believe."

Now a week later his disciples were again inside and Thomas was with them. Jesus came, although the doors were locked, and stood in their midst and said, "Peace be with you." Then he said to Thomas, "Put your finger here and see my hands, and bring your hand and put it into my side, and do not be unbelieving, but believe." Thomas answered and said to him, "My Lord and my God!" Jesus said to him, "Have you come to believe because you have seen me? Blessed are those who have not seen and have believed."

Reflecting on the Word

Both Resurrection appearances occurred on the first day of the week, which eventually became our Sunday. Jesus' appearances were certainly miracles. Thomas was the only disciple missing at Jesus' first appearance, and he believed when Jesus appeared for the second time. We can identify with Thomas' unbelief, because we can often doubt the presence of God in our lives. It is appropriate this Sunday to welcome and contemplate the great mystery that is Easter.

...... ON THE WAY TO MASS:

I wonder if the family understands the new life that Easter brings. What do colored eggs mean at Easter Time?

ON THE WAY HOME FROM MASS: ......

With faith, we can believe in Resurrection. If you were Thomas, how would you have reacted to seeing Jesus?

Living the Word

The season of Easter is meant to be lived in a mood of great joy. Longer days with more daylight approach, and it may be time to do some planting—again, new life. The younger children can seed and sow grass, while the older ones may start seedlings that will eventually be transplanted into the warm ground for a garden. Keep the "alleluia" hello active in your home. Take time over the next four days for a family reading of the the *Exsultet*, a lyric poem that the deacon or priest sings at the Easter Vigil.

April 30, 2017

Third Sunday of Easter

Hearing the Word

Luke 24:13–15, 30–32

In the name of the Father, and of the Son, and of the Holy Spirit.

That very day, the first day of the week, two of Jesus' disciples were going to a village seven miles from Jerusalem called Emmaus, and they were conversing about all the things that had occurred. And it happened that while they were conversing and debating, Jesus himself drew near and walked with them. And it happened that, while he was with them at table, he took bread, said the blessing, broke it, and gave it to them. With that their eyes were opened and they recognized him, but he vanished from their sight. Then they said to each other, "Were not our hearts burning within us while he spoke to us on the way and opened the Scriptures to us?"

Reflecting on the Word

In Luke's account of the journey to Emmaus, the Risen Jesus joins the disciples as they walk along the road. The disciples only recognize him in the breaking of the bread. This story has more than one theme. We hear of the disciples' hospitality as they invite Jesus to dine with them. Jesus blesses the bread, breaks it, and gives it to the disciples. With this, their eyes were opened and they recognized him. How does the Eucharist open your eyes?

...... ON THE WAY TO MASS:

Have you ever met someone, and immediately known that you wanted to befriend that person?

ON THE WAY HOME FROM MASS: ......

Jesus is with us, but differently than in the Gospel story. How is Jesus alive and among us today?

Living the Word

We have lived another Lent, and now we are in a great "procession" through the season of Easter to the time of eventual eternity. Talk about processions with the family: are they formal or informal? Do people carry things in a procession? Do processions have or need music? Next Sunday, find and name the four processions that happen during the Mass. (Hint: Entrance procession, procession with the gifts, Communion procession, Recessional procession.) Take a springtime walk (mute the electronic devices) and make it a procession in search of the new life of spring.

May 7, 2017

Fourth Sunday of Easter

Hearing the Word

John 10:1–10

In the name of the Father, and of the Son, and of the Holy Spirit.

Jesus said: "Amen, amen, I say to you, whoever does not enter a sheepfold through the gate but climbs over elsewhere is a thief and a robber. But whoever enters through the gate is the shepherd of the sheep. The gatekeeper opens it for him, and the sheep hear his voice, as the shepherd calls his own sheep by name and leads them out. When he has driven out all his own, he walks ahead of them, and the sheep follow him, because they recognize his voice. But they will not follow a stranger; they will run away from him, because they do not recognize the voice of strangers." Although Jesus used this figure of speech, the Pharisees did not realize what he was trying to tell them.

So Jesus said again, "Amen, amen, I say to you, I am the gate for the sheep. All who came before me are thieves and robbers, but the sheep did not listen to them. I am the gate. Whoever enters through me will be saved, and will come in and go out and find pasture. A thief comes only to steal and slaughter and destroy; I came so that they might have life and have it more abundantly."

Reflecting on the Word

The Fourth Sunday of Easter is known as Good Shepherd Sunday since each year the Gospel likens the care Jesus has for us to that of a shepherd for his sheep. Today's Gospel indicates that anyone who would enter the sheep pen by climbing over the gate is not a real shepherd. The authentic shepherd uses the gate, knows the names of his sheep, and leads them in a beneficial direction. The leadership of the authentic shepherd is effective because the shepherd's voice is known. Jesus also compares himself to a gate: if you are a believer, you will receive "abundant life" through this gate.

...... ON THE WAY TO MASS:

We live in a world full of noisy distractions. How can we hear the voice of Jesus in our lives?

ON THE WAY HOME FROM MASS: ......

Who has led you somewhere, and then something good has happened to you? What do good leaders do?

Living the Word

As the family spring cleans, members can make it a family project to decide on possessions that can be given to the needy. To observe the holiness of Sunday, schedule cleaning for midweek or Saturday afternoon after sports. Before making a trip to the donation center, have the children help fill a box for the local food pantry. It's May, so plan time each Sunday for praying the Rosary with the family. Consider inviting the neighbors to pray and share supper.

May 14, 2017

Fifth Sunday of Easter

Hearing the Word

John 14:1–10a

In the name of the Father, and of the Son, and of the Holy Spirit.

Jesus said to his disciples: "Do not let your hearts be troubled. You have faith in God; have faith also in me. In my Father's house there are many dwelling places. If there were not, would I have told you that I am going to prepare a place for you? And if I go and prepare a place for you, I will come back again and take you to myself, so that where I am you also may be. Where I am going you know the way." Thomas said to him, "Master, we do not know where you are going; how can we know the way?" Jesus said to him, "I am the way and the truth and the life. No one comes to the Father except through me. If you know me, then you will also know my Father. From now on you do know him and have seen him." Philip said to him, "Master, show us the Father, and that will be enough for us." Jesus said to him, "Have I been with you for so long a time and you still do not know me, Philip? Whoever has seen me has seen the Father. How can you say, 'Show us the Father'? Do you not believe that I am in the Father and the Father is in me?"

Reflecting on the Word

Apostles Thomas and Philip are questioning Jesus, and Jesus is reassuring and tender. Jesus encourages trust in his teachings, and gives hope for the future. The Apostles have a hint that Jesus will not be with them much longer, as he describes his Father's house as having many dwelling places. If the Apostles believe that Jesus is the "way," then they know that he is the path toward salvation. And how wonderful the promise that the Apostles would perform even greater miracles than Jesus!

...... ON THE WAY TO MASS:

As Christians, our family is part of the community that Jesus left on earth. How do we mirror what Jesus taught?

ON THE WAY HOME FROM MASS: ......

Do we belong to a parish community that shares the Good News? How do you know this?

Living the Word

Remind the family that Jesus promised us that he would wait for us in heaven. We need to spread the Good News while we wait here on earth. What is the Good News today? Each day this week, have a member of the family share some Good (Gospel) News. Make a refrigerator chart and share the news! An example would be, "I was a Christian when I (did my homework without complaining, picked up my toys without being told, complimented someone at school, brought coffee to a stressed coworker). Small "messages" of good news add up!

May 21, 2017

Sixth Sunday of Easter

Hearing the Word

John 14:15–21

In the name of the Father, and of the Son, and of the Holy Spirit.

Jesus said to his disciples: "If you love me, you will keep my commandments. And I will ask the Father, and he will give you another Advocate to be with you always, the Spirit of truth, whom the world cannot accept, because it neither sees nor knows him. But you know him, because he remains with you, and will be in you. I will not leave you orphans; I will come to you. In a little while the world will no longer see me, but you will see me, because I live and you will live. On that day you will realize that I am in my Father and you are in me and I in you. Whoever has my commandments and observes them is the one who loves me. And whoever loves me will be loved by my Father, and I will love him and reveal myself to him."

Reflecting on the Word

The advocacy of the Holy Spirit is a special gift that Jesus shares with us. The continuation of the reading of John 14 from last Sunday provides riches nearly beyond belief, as Jesus promises to live on if we love him by loving one another. Although people today struggle with overemphasis on material wealth and are sidetracked by electronic distractions, keeping the Commandments is the key to staying with and in God. If we love the Father, we are shaped and supported by the Holy Spirit who is with us always.

......ON THE WAY TO MASS:

I wonder if our family can recognize the movement of the Holy Spirit. What does the Holy Spirit do?

ON THE WAY HOME FROM MASS: ......

The Holy Spirit gives us support and comforts us with grace. Do we often look to the Holy Spirit for help?

Living the Word

The love that comes to us from the Holy Spirit is the life that Jesus wants us to share with others. During the Sacrament of Confirmation, the bishop lays hands on an individual and prays that the Holy Spirit will help them love God and share goodness. Make a goodness basket together: dye several eggs, add touches of hard candy, maybe some tea bags, and even a loaf of bread or some coupons. Share unexpected goodness with a teacher, a coworker, or a neighbor who lives alone.

May 25, 2017

Solemnity of the Ascension of the Lord

Hearing the Word

Matthew 28:16–20

In the name of the Father, and of the Son, and of the Holy Spirit.

The eleven disciples went to Galilee, to the mountain to which Jesus had ordered them. When they saw him, they worshiped, but they doubted. Then Jesus approached and said to them, "All power in heaven and on earth has been given to me. Go, therefore, and make disciples of all nations, baptizing them in the name of the Father, and of the Son, and of the Holy Spirit, teaching them to observe all that I have commanded you. And behold, I am with you always, until the end of the age."

Reflecting on the Word

What a farewell speech Jesus offered his followers! Before Jesus leaves "the eleven disciples," he commissions them for ministry. Their mission is to "make disciples of all nations." This truly is evangelization rooted in the support of the Holy Spirit. As Catholic Christians, we believe that Jesus ascended into heaven with his body, leaving a community of believers to spread the Good News on earth. The new "body" of Christ was that fledgling Christian community, led by the Apostles.

......ON THE WAY TO MASS:

Have you ever felt a little unready and insecure, yet confident about doing something new?

ON THE WAY HOME FROM MASS: ......

Jesus left his followers with hope and the Holy Spirit. Do we still have this hope for life with Jesus?

Living the Word

As a family, dramatically proclaim Matthew's Gospel, chapter 28. There is plenty of action and characters for a family drama: the angel, the women, the guards, Jesus, the chief priests, the Apostles. Have the best reader proclaim this Gospel and designate others to pantomime the characters as it is read. Use the family living area or the yard for the stage.

May 28, 2017

Seventh Sunday of Easter

Hearing the Word

John 17:1–11a

In the name of the Father, and of the Son, and of the Holy Spirit.

Jesus raised his eyes to heaven and said, "Father, the hour has come. Give glory to your son, so that your son may glorify you, just as you gave him authority over all people, so that your son may give eternal life to all you gave him. Now this is eternal life, that they should know you, the only true God, and the one whom you sent, Jesus Christ. I glorified you on earth by accomplishing the work that you gave me to do. Now glorify me, Father, with you, with the glory that I had with you before the world began.

"I revealed your name to those whom you gave me out of the world. They belonged to you, and you gave them to me, and they have kept your word. Now they know that everything you gave me is from you, because the words you gave to me I have given to them, and they accepted them and truly understood that I came from you, and they have believed that you sent me. I pray for them. I do not pray for the world but for the ones you have given me, because they are yours, and everything of mine is yours and everything of yours is mine, and I have been glorified in them. And now I will no longer be in the world, but they are in the world, while I am coming to you."

Reflecting on the Word

Jesus provides an eloquent farewell message, before his agony in the garden. He speaks tenderly to God, and he talks about their relationship as divine beings. It is evident that Jesus wants to return to the glory that was once his, shared with the Father and the Holy Spirit. The last Sunday of Easter demonstrates to us that we live today in the already-but-the-not-yet: we live in tension between our flawed human nature and the need for God to provide eternal salvation. Jesus' prayer resonates this reality.

•••••• ON THE WAY TO MASS:

We close the season of Easter soon. Could we plant a family garden this year, during our Easter springtime?

ON THE WAY HOME FROM MASS: ••••••

Sowing and sprouting for Jesus, we are gardeners for God. How can we grow and harvest followers?

Living the Word

As a family, plan and plant a garden. Consider container gardening if you have limited space. Don't hesitate to plow some of your grass and make room for new life. Grandparents can be helpful in nurturing the seedlings. Invite extended family to join the effort. Community gardens build positive impressions for children, feeding our families and tending the fragile environment. Bless the garden as you plant and give praise to God for the harvest later on. Sing the refrain of "We Are Called" (D. Haas, GIA Publications, Inc.).

June 4, 2017

Pentecost Sunday

Hearing the Word

John 20:19–23

In the name of the Father, and of the Son, and of the Holy Spirit.

On the evening of that first day of the week, when the doors were locked, where the disciples were, for fear of the Jews, Jesus came and stood in their midst and said to them, "Peace be with you." When he had said this, he showed them his hands and his side. The disciples rejoiced when they saw the Lord. Jesus said to them again, "Peace be with you. As the Father has sent me, so I send you." And when he had said this, he breathed on them and said to them, "Receive the Holy Spirit. Whose sins you forgive are forgiven them, and whose sins you retain are retained."

Reflecting on the Word

There was awe but probably fear, too, when Jesus appeared to his disciples, despite locked doors. We take note of Jesus' greeting, "Peace be with you," because the disciples were so troubled about the Jews. It resonates with hope for good health, prosperity, and calmness. The image of Jesus breathing on the disciples is reminiscent of the "holy breathing" that the bishop does when he consecrates the chrism every year. That "breath" represents the indwelling of God, breaking into our present.

......ON THE WAY TO MASS:

We celebrate the descent of the Holy Spirit at Pentecost. How can we open our hearts to the Holy Spirit?

ON THE WAY HOME FROM MASS: ......

Imagine the huge gathering of diverse people at Pentecost. Why is there so little peace among cultures today?

Living the Word

Gather the family to prepare Pentecost cookies or cupcakes today. Red is the liturgical color for the day, so the cupcakes could be covered with red frosting. Pentecost is a day of images of wind and fire. (The breath of God is the wind, and the tongues of fire appeared over the disciples' heads.) Let the children create outdoor streamers with colored tissue or purchase pinwheels for everyone. Decorate the porch or yard with a windsock or a billowy fabric that catches the wind and supports the image. Encourage everyone to wear clothing that is "Pentecost red."

June 11, 2017

Solemnity of the Most Holy Trinity

Hearing the Word

John 3:16–18

In the name of the Father, and of the Son, and of the Holy Spirit.

God so loved the world that he gave his only Son, so that everyone who believes in him might not perish but might have eternal life. For God did not send his Son into the world to condemn the world, but that the world might be saved through him. Whoever believes in him will not be condemned, but whoever does not believe has already been condemned, because he has not believed in the name of the only Son of God.

Reflecting on the Word

These Scripture verses relate part of a dialogue that Jesus was having with a Pharisee named Nicodemus. Nicodemus "came at night" (verse 2) and wondered if God was indeed "with" Jesus, based on the signs and miracles that he had heard about. Jesus advises the man that belief in the Son of God is the basis for being saved. Conversely, unbelief in the Son of God results in a judgment against that person. The conversation ends with Jesus' teaching rather than Nicodemus' conversion.

...... ON THE WAY TO MASS:

Today is Trinity Sunday. How would you explain the Father, the Son, and the Holy Spirit to a friend?

ON THE WAY HOME FROM MASS: ......

God sent Jesus to save the world. That means everyone, right? How can you help save the world today?

Living the Word

We think of the blessed Trinity as "three" because of the connection of the Father, the Son, and the Holy Spirit. Trinity Sunday suggests a "trinity day" at home. Engage your children in doing as many things as you can in a series of "threes": eat three tacos, say "I love you" to someone three times, play three card games. As you do this, remember how much God loves us. God sent his Son Jesus, followed by the Holy Spirit for ages unending. Find and show the children a church in your state or city that is named after the Holy Trinity.

June 18, 2017

Solemnity of the Most Holy Body and Blood of Christ

Hearing the Word

John 6:51–58

In the name of the Father, and of the Son, and of the Holy Spirit.

Jesus said to the Jewish crowds: "I am the living bread that came down from heaven; whoever eats this bread will live forever; and the bread that I will give is my flesh for the life of the world."

The Jews quarreled among themselves, saying, "How can this man give us his flesh to eat?" Jesus said to them, "Amen, amen, I say to you, unless you eat the flesh of the Son of Man and drink his blood, you do not have life within you. Whoever eats my flesh and drinks my blood has eternal life, and I will raise him on the last day. For my flesh is true food, and my blood is true drink. Whoever eats my flesh and drinks my blood remains in me and I in him. Just as the living Father sent me and I have life because of the Father, so also the one who feeds on me will have life because of me. This is the bread that came down from heaven. Unlike your ancestors who ate and still died, whoever eats this bread will live forever."

Reflecting on the Word

We can only live forever if we eat Jesus' "Flesh" and drink his "Blood." This discourse of John's on the Bread of Life points to the life that receiving the Eucharist provides to us. "Feeding" on Jesus comments on his sacrifice on the Cross, and our celebration of this sacrifice at Mass. We are invited to receive Holy Communion in its "fuller form" of consecrated bread and wine. Jesus expects us to become what we eat, so that we can truly live forever.

......ON THE WAY TO MASS:

If we eat Jesus' Body and drink his Blood, we will live forever. Why would anyone not receive Communion?

ON THE WAY HOME FROM MASS: ......

Would you miss receiving Communion if it wasn't offered every week during Mass? For younger children: Why do you look forward to receiving Communion?

Living the Word

Sing the refrain of the song "One Bread, One Body" (J. Foley, OCP). Discover the prayer Anima Christi and share it with family members. Composed around the fourteenth century, this prayer is most often used as a thanksgiving prayer after receiving the Body and Blood of Christ. Some people memorized this prayer as children, and still remember it as adults. Receiving Jesus' Body and Blood can transform us.

June 25, 2017

Twelfth Sunday in Ordinary Time

Hearing the Word

Matthew 10:26–33

In the name of the Father, and of the Son, and of the Holy Spirit.

Jesus said to the Twelve: "Fear no one. Nothing is concealed that will not be revealed, nor secret that will not be known. What I say to you in the darkness, speak in the light; what you hear whispered, proclaim on the housetops. And do not be afraid of those who kill the body but cannot kill the soul; rather, be afraid of the one who can destroy both soul and body in Gehenna. Are not two sparrows sold for a small coin? Yet not one of them falls to the ground without your Father's knowledge. Even all the hairs of your head are counted. So do not be afraid; you are worth more than many sparrows. Everyone who acknowledges me before others I will acknowledge before my heavenly Father. But whoever denies me before others, I will deny before my heavenly Father."

Reflecting on the Word

Jesus is giving instructions to his Apostles, especially regarding how to live openly in God's love. He also stresses the wisdom of God, "even all the hairs of your head are counted." Unlike popular Jewish belief at that time, Jesus assures the Twelve that they should shift to being bold (that is, "speak in the light") and without fear (that is, "fear" God but no others). It's not difficult to believe that, if God cares for the tiny sparrows, he will also care for us. Nothing is inconsequential with God.

...... ON THE WAY TO MASS:

God loves us, no matter what we do. What signs do you see that God cares for us daily?

ON THE WAY HOME FROM MASS: ......

What special signs of God's love do we see as we travel home from Mass today?

Living the Word

No matter what the family's school schedule, everyone should enjoy some down time during the summer. Set aside some time with your children to use the gift of play and of delight that God has given you. Seek also to help a neighbor or family member with an act of kindness. Concentrate on appreciating the beauty of nature as a family this summer.

July 2, 2017

Thirteenth Sunday in Ordinary Time

Hearing the Word

Matthew 10:37–42

In the name of the Father, and of the Son, and of the Holy Spirit.

Jesus said to his apostles: "Whoever loves father or mother more than me is not worthy of me and whoever loves son or daughter more than me is not worthy of me; and whoever does not take up his cross and follow after me is not worthy of me. Whoever finds his life will lose it, and whoever loses his life for my sake will find it.

"Whoever receives you receives me, and whoever receives me receives the one who sent me. Whoever receives a prophet because he is a prophet will receive a prophet's reward, and whoever receives a righteous man because he is a righteous man will receive a righteous man's reward. And whoever gives only a cup of cold water to one of these little ones to drink because the little one is a disciple—amen, I say to you, he will surely not lose his reward."

Reflecting on the Word

Jesus is empowering his disciples for ministry. Matthew's community was being persecuted at the time. Jewish Christians were not welcome in the synagogues, so discipleship came with a cost. Today's Gospel challenges all disciples to make a serious commitment to living the Gospel as Jesus wanted. Notice how Matthew talks about how to treat a prophet. Being hospitable to a prophet was a radically different notion, because in biblical times, prophets were usually killed if they spread unpopular ideas.

...... ON THE WAY TO MASS:

As a family, have we opened our door in hospitality to anyone recently? How could we do this?

ON THE WAY HOME FROM MASS: ......

God promised to be with us always, after Jesus ascended to heaven. Where can we look to find God's presence?

Living the Word

Since a national holiday approaches, let's roll out the "hospitality red carpet" (find an inexpensive rug or make one with heavy paper) and invite another family to share faith, food, and fun. Take a few minutes to talk about "why we feel welcome at church on Sunday," pray, and then eat. It's helpful to notice, too, if your parish welcomes children at liturgy, people who are disabled, and those who seem out of place (prophets?) in daily life. Does your parish provide child care for adult events?

July 9, 2017

Fourteenth Sunday in Ordinary Time

Hearing the Word

Matthew 11:25–30

In the name of the Father, and of the Son, and of the Holy Spirit.

At that time Jesus exclaimed: "I give praise to you, Father, Lord of heaven and earth, for although you have hidden these things from the wise and the learned you have revealed them to little ones. Yes, Father, such has been your gracious will. All things have been handed over to me by my Father. No one knows the Son except the Father, and no one knows the Father except the Son and anyone to whom the Son wishes to reveal him.

"Come to me, all you who labor and are burdened, and I will give you rest. Take my yoke upon you and learn from me, for I am meek and humble of heart; and you will find rest for yourselves. For my yoke is easy, and my burden light."

Reflecting on the Word

Jesus is God's mystery, and he explains himself in terms of how he relates to the Father. Jesus exclaims that the little ones who receive wisdom are those who are humble and accept faith. The invitation, "Come to me," invites us to a childlike faith that offers peace, rest, and a life of harmony. The yoke of Pharisaic law was heavy and difficult to observe, in Jesus' time. Jesus teaches that if you take his "yoke," you can live freely without fear of reprisal.

...... ON THE WAY TO MASS:

The Gospel says that children understand faith easier than grown-ups. Can you share a teaching of Jesus?

ON THE WAY HOME FROM MASS: ......

What was the "yoke" that Jesus was asking us to put on our shoulders? What is a burden in our lives?

Living the Word

In the coming week, pick one time that you could have a family meal. Read Matthew 11:25–30 as the meal prayer, and at the end of the meal, invite family members to respond to the questions: What does God ask of me in my life? Does God intend for us to do really hard things? Why should life be a burden if we have God with us? This Gospel is a reading that invites a response from its listeners, regardless of age. Faith gives all of us eyes to see what we need to do to get to heaven.

July 16, 2017

Fifteenth Sunday in Ordinary Time

Hearing the Word

Matthew 13:1–9

In the name of the Father, and of the Son, and of the Holy Spirit.

On that day, Jesus went out of the house and sat down by the sea. Such large crowds gathered around him that he got into a boat and sat down, and the whole crowd stood along the shore. And he spoke to them at length in parables, saying: "A sower went out to sow. And as he sowed, some seed fell on the path, and birds came and ate it up. Some fell on rocky ground, where it had little soil. It sprang up at once because the soil was not deep, and when the sun rose it was scorched, and it withered for lack of roots. Some seed fell among thorns, and the thorns grew up and choked it. But some seed fell on rich soil, and produced fruit, a hundred or sixty or thirtyfold. Whoever has ears ought to hear."

Reflecting on the Word

Jesus often spoke in parables, since this was a way to get people's attention. A parable always contains a "nugget" that hooks the listener into the meaning. The hook in this Gospel is the condition of the soil. Sometimes the Good News is presented and it is ignored, like the seed falling on rocky ground. How useless to plant seed on rocks! The audience probably responded and understood that the rich soil could exist within their hearts, if they were ready to receive the Word of God.

...... ON THE WAY TO MASS:

Does our family understand what a parable is? What movie with an unexpected ending have you seen?

ON THE WAY HOME FROM MASS: ......

Jesus didn't hide from people who wanted to hear him speak. Do we hide if we think Jesus is speaking to us?

Living the Word

It's easy to ignore God in our lives. We have ears to hear and eyes to see, but sometimes we don't want to hear Jesus in our minds. Plan for a family day away from all electronics. During this day, send each person outside for five minutes, and meet up in a designated place together. Encourage eyes to "see" and ears to "hear." (Go to the mall if it's raining.) Then gather together and discover if anyone "saw" or "heard" God's voice.

July 23, 2016

Sixteenth Sunday in Ordinary Time

Hearing the Word

Matthew 13:24–30

In the name of the Father, and of the Son, and of the Holy Spirit.

Jesus proposed another parable to the crowds, saying: "The kingdom of heaven may be likened to a man who sowed good seed in his field. While everyone was asleep his enemy came and sowed weeds all through the wheat, and then went off. When the crop grew and bore fruit, the weeds appeared as well. The slaves of the householder came to him and said, 'Master, did you not sow good seed in your field? Where have the weeds come from?' He answered, 'An enemy has done this.' His slaves said to him, 'Do you want us to go and pull them up?' He replied, 'No, if you pull up the weeds you might uproot the wheat along with them. Let them grow together until harvest; then at harvest time I will say to the harvesters, "First collect the weeds and tie them in bundles for burning; but gather the wheat into my barn."'"

Reflecting on the Word

Jesus' parables seem to captivate the people who must grow things in order to live. Allowing wheat and weeds to grow at the same time until harvest is like good people and sinners being together in the world. In eternity, Jesus will welcome the good and "bundle for burning" those who have not been faithful followers. It's terrifying to think of being bundled for eternal condemnation, but the greater question is "where have the weeds come from?" The weeds are unrepentant people who made sinful choices.

...... ON THE WAY TO MASS:

Have you experienced a time when you did something that you thought that God would never forgive?

ON THE WAY HOME FROM MASS: ......

Weeds will always be weeds; they will never become flowers or fruit. Are we like weeds if we disobey God?

Living the Word

We believe in a God who loves us unconditionally. We are God's children through Baptism. Even though evil exists in the world and bad things happen sometimes, God forgives our sins and welcomes us into heaven. We need to aim our lives on God, and stay focused on loving God and each other. Find a morning or evening Mass in your neighborhood this week, and attend as a family. Receive Holy Communion joyfully, and give thanks to God for his unconditional love.

July 30, 2017

Seventeenth Sunday in Ordinary Time

Hearing the Word

Matthew 13:44–52

In the name of the Father, and of the Son, and of the Holy Spirit.

Jesus said to his disciples: "The kingdom of heaven is like a treasure buried in a field, which a person finds and hides again, and out of joy goes and sells all that he has and buys that field." Again, the kingdom of heaven is like a merchant searching for fine pearls. When he finds a pearl of great price, he goes and sells all that he has and buys it. "Again, the kingdom of heaven is like a net thrown into the sea, which collects fish of every kind. When it is full they haul it ashore and sit down to put what is good into buckets. What is bad they throw away. Thus it will be at the end of the age. The angels will go out and separate the wicked from the righteous and throw them into the fiery furnace, where there will be wailing and grinding of teeth.

"Do you understand all these things?" They answered, "Yes." And he replied, "Then every scribe who has been instructed in the kingdom of heaven is like the head of a household who brings from his storeroom both the new and the old."

Reflecting on the Word

Jesus uses the image of a pearl of great price, a treasure in a field, and a catch of fish to explain the Kingdom of Heaven. Through these images, the disciples learn how priceless is the Kingdom of Heaven. If the Kingdom of Heaven is priceless, should not we do all that we can to nurture and protect our faith? What would you liken the Kingdom of Heaven to? How do you nourish your faith so that at the end of the age, you will be with the righteous?

...... ON THE WAY TO MASS:

God is truly more generous than we will ever know. How has God been generous to you?

ON THE WAY HOME FROM MASS: ......

When you go to heaven, what treasure would you thank God for? Is heaven a gift or a reward?

Living the Word

Understanding what Jesus wants us to do isn't easy sometimes. It's easier to be good if you remember that in life you will make mistakes. All mistakes are not sins. In fact, very few mistakes are sins. Pretend that you played all afternoon with a friend and forgot to clean your messy room. Your dad says, "You made a big mistake and disobeyed our rule about cleaning your room on Saturday." Then God appears: "Just say you are sorry, and admit that you made a mistake. You didn't sin, you just forgot. Now get busy!"

August 6, 2017

Transfiguration of the Lord

Hearing the Word

Matthew 17:1–9

In the name of the Father, and of the Son, and of the Holy Spirit.

Jesus took Peter, James, and his brother, John, and led them up a high mountain by themselves. And he was transfigured before them; his face shone like the sun and his clothes became white as light. And behold, Moses and Elijah appeared to them, conversing with him. Then Peter said to Jesus in reply, "Lord, it is good that we are here. If you wish, I will make three tents here, one for you, one for Moses, and one for Elijah." While he was still speaking, behold, a bright cloud cast a shadow over them, then from the cloud came a voice that said, "This is my beloved Son, with whom I am well pleased; listen to him." When the disciples heard this, they fell prostrate and were very much afraid. But Jesus came and touched them, saying, "Rise, and do not be afraid." And when the disciples raised their eyes, they saw no one else but Jesus alone.

As they were coming down from the mountain, Jesus charged them, "Do not tell the vision to anyone until the Son of Man has been raised from the dead."

Reflecting on the Word

This Gospel grabs our attention immediately: Jesus' face "shone like the sun" and "his clothes became white as light." Can you imagine the squinting, terrified disciples? Recall that the prophets foretold this Transfiguration, this visual revelation to the three disciples that Jesus was truly God. How amazing, frightening, and wonderful that Jesus showed his glory before he ever died on the Cross. How much better could the Apostles proclaim his message, having seen the glorified Jesus!

...... ON THE WAY TO MASS:

What's the most amazing movie you ever saw about someone or something that is changed into something else?

ON THE WAY HOME FROM MASS: ......

Put yourself on top of that mountain with Jesus and the three Apostles. What do you think the Apostles really saw?

Living the Word

Plan a Transfiguration breakfast or supper with the family. Transform raw eggs into scrambled eggs, bread into toast, raw meat into crunchy bacon, dough into pizza crust, apples into applesauce. Get the entire family to think of other things that can be "transfigured" to make it easier to understand that Jesus was still Jesus but he was changed on the mountain: the Son of Man became the Son of God. We know that Jesus will return for us in glory because the Apostles saw him resurrected.

August 13, 2017

Nineteenth Sunday in Ordinary Time

Hearing the Word

Matthew 14:22–33

In the name of the Father, and of the Son, and of the Holy Spirit.

After he had fed the people, Jesus made the disciples get into a boat and precede him to the other side, while he dismissed the crowds. After doing so, he went up on the mountain by himself to pray. When it was evening he was there alone. Meanwhile the boat, already a few miles offshore, was being tossed about by the waves, for the wind was against it. During the fourth watch of the night, he came toward them walking on the sea. When the disciples saw him walking on the sea they were terrified. "It is a ghost," they said, and they cried out in fear. At once Jesus spoke to them, "Take courage, it is I; do not be afraid." Peter said to him in reply, "Lord, if it is you, command me to come to you on the water." He said, "Come." Peter got out of the boat and began to walk on the water toward Jesus. But when he saw how strong the wind was he became frightened; and, beginning to sink, he cried out, "Lord, save me!" Immediately Jesus stretched out his hand and caught Peter, and said to him, "O you of little faith, why did you doubt?" After they got into the boat, the wind died down. Those who were in the boat did him homage, saying, "Truly, you are the Son of God."

Reflecting on the Word

What a wondrous story about how faith makes a difference in our lives! When Peter had courageous faith, he managed to walk on water. When his faith wavered, he needed Jesus to support him. Often, life is much like this stormy boat ride. We forget God, we panic at life's challenges, and we quickly think that we're drowning. Doubt makes us feel hopeless, and faith nurtures and shapes a brave response. Jesus always stretches out his hand, ready with mercy and hope. Faith trumps fear.

...... ON THE WAY TO MASS:

Have you ever had an experience that felt like God was whispering to you and was somehow with you?

ON THE WAY HOME FROM MASS: ......

If life seems to fall apart, we need Jesus. How do you get in touch with Jesus if you are having a problem?

Living the Word

Jesus gave Peter his hand as Peter was falling into the water. With your children, talk briefly about the expression "to give a helping hand." Ask everyone to think of at least one person to offer a hand to this week. Trace around each hand in the family, and cut out the shape. Keep the "hands" in a bowl on the counter. As each person comes home every day, ask if they've given someone a helping hand on that day. If so, tape their "hand" cutout to the fridge or in a window for all to see.

August 15, 2017

Solemnity of the Assumption of the Blessed Virgin Mary

Hearing the Word

Luke 1:39–55

In the name of the Father, and of the Son, and of the Holy Spirit.

Mary set out and traveled to the hill country in haste to a town of Judah, where she entered the house of Zechariah and greeted Elizabeth. When Elizabeth heard Mary's greeting, the infant leaped in her womb, and Elizabeth, filled with the Holy Spirit, cried out in a loud voice and said, "Blessed are you among women, and blessed is the fruit of your womb."

And Mary said:

"My soul proclaims the greatness of the Lord; / my spirit rejoices in God my Savior / for he has looked with favor on his lowly servant. / From this day all generations will call me blessed: / the Almighty has done great things for me / and holy is his Name. / He has mercy on those who fear him / in every generation. / He has shown the strength of his arm, / and has scattered the proud in their conceit. / He has cast down the mighty from their thrones, / and has lifted up the lowly. / He has filled the hungry with good things, / and the rich he has sent away empty. / He has come to the help of his servant Israel / for he has remembered his promise of mercy, / the promise he made to our fathers, / to Abraham and his children forever."

Reflecting on the Word

When Mary visited Elizabeth, she wanted to share her good news. Her cousin, with the Holy Spirit's help, welcomed her, and at the same time, felt her baby move. Realizing how blessed she was by God, Mary proclaimed a poem that we still sing and recite. Her *Magnificat* sings praise for the goodness of God and the fulfillment of the promise that God made to Abraham.

...... ON THE WAY TO MASS:

We will hear a wonderful story about Mary being pregnant with Jesus. Listen and find out how God made Mary happy and joyful.

ON THE WAY HOME FROM MASS: ......

What if Jesus had been born into our family, instead of to Mary? What would we say to our friends? How would we plan to rejoice?

Living the Word

Find a time this week to remind the family to be joyful and grateful for the good things that happen. Make two pans of brownies or a favorite bar cookie: one pan of brownies will be unfrosted, while the other will not only have frosting but will be decorated with candy. The fancy treats show what life feels like when everything goes our way. Though the other batch of brownies lack candy, they still taste good. Life with God can be "one pan or the other," but we can still find joy—as Mary did—in the gifts that God sends to us.

August 20, 2017

Twentieth Sunday in Ordinary Time

Hearing the Word

Matthew 15:21–28

In the name of the Father, and of the Son, and of the Holy Spirit.

At that time, Jesus withdrew to the region of Tyre and Sidon. And behold, a Canaanite woman of that district came and called out, "Have pity on me, Lord, Son of David! My daughter is tormented by a demon." But Jesus did not say a word in answer to her. Jesus' disciples came and asked him, "Send her away, for she keeps calling out after us." He said in reply, "I was sent only to the lost sheep of the house of Israel." But the woman came and did Jesus homage, saying, "Lord, help me." He said in reply, "It is not right to take the food of the children and throw it to the dogs." She said, "Please, Lord, for even the dogs eat the scraps that fall from the table of their masters." Then Jesus said to her in reply, "O woman, great is your faith! Let it be done for you as you wish." And the woman's daughter was healed from that hour.

Reflecting on the Word

In Jesus' time, people believed that evil spirits prowled around, and the person who had the more powerful spirit could control a less powerful spirit. The woman found Jesus and asked that he control the tormenter of her daughter. Jesus didn't ignore her, but rather he waited to see if she would express faith rather than seem to be chasing him as a magical healer. The woman's faith, and Jesus' patience, won the day for her daughter. This Canaanite woman didn't seem to have a chance, but Jesus welcomed her faith.

...... ON THE WAY TO MASS:

What if you need healing in mind or body, and God doesn't give it to you?

ON THE WAY HOME FROM MASS: ......

We expect Jesus to provide healing for everyone who asks. Does God really reject us for asking?

Living the Word

God always hears what we ask, in prayer, and sends the healing that we need. Sometimes we don't recognize this healing; sometimes we don't even accept what God sends. Read the Gospel aloud again and help the children imagine that the woman followed Jesus for two hours and begged for healing for her daughter. Sometimes in life, we have to be as focused and persistent as this woman was with Jesus. We have to have a persistent faith in God. Jesus, give us patience and persistence!

August 27, 2017

Twenty-First Sunday in Ordinary Time

Hearing the Word

Matthew 16:13–20

In the name of the Father, and of the Son, and of the Holy Spirit.

Jesus went into the region of Caesarea Philippi and he asked his disciples, "Who do people say that the Son of Man is?" They replied, "Some say John the Baptist, others Elijah, still others Jeremiah or one of the prophets." He said to them, "But who do you say that I am?" Simon Peter said in reply, "You are the Christ, the Son of the living God." Jesus said to him in reply, "Blessed are you, Simon son of Jonah. For flesh and blood has not revealed this to you, but my heavenly Father. And so I say to you, you are Peter, and upon this rock I will build my church, and the gates of the netherworld shall not prevail against it. I will give you the keys to the kingdom of heaven. Whatever you bind on earth shall be bound in heaven; and whatever you loose on earth shall be loosed in heaven." Then he strictly ordered his disciples to tell no one that he was the Christ.

Reflecting on the Word

Jesus offers Peter leadership based on the affirmation that Peter knew Jesus was the "Son of the living God." Peter knew this, despite his early failure to trust Jesus and his inability to recognize Jesus as God. Jesus rewarded Peter with the authority to enforce laws and to loosen the bonds that laws also can provide. Recall that Peter was among the first Apostles whom Jesus called, and he was the person named to "feed my sheep." Peter is recognized as the first pope.

...... ON THE WAY TO MASS:

Can you think of some world and Church leaders whom Jesus would reward today?

ON THE WAY HOME FROM MASS: ......

We can be leaders of God's people because we have been baptized. How can we tell if our leaders have faith?

Living the Word

Jesus gave us the authority to be leaders and do ministry in his name. Ask the children what a servant is, and then ask what a leader does. Write out some ideas about both on a tablet, so that they can follow the logic of becoming a servant-leader. Pope Francis wants us to do exactly that. He wants us to be humble and helpful, and to invite others to join us. This is called "evangelization." Make "evangelization" the Word of the Week. Write as many words as you can with the letters in "evangelization."

Everyday Family Prayers

The Sign of the Cross

The Sign of the Cross is the first prayer and the last: of each day, and of each Christian life. It is a prayer of the body as well as a prayer of words. When we are presented for Baptism, the community traces this sign on our bodies for the first time. Parents may trace it daily on their children. We learn to trace it daily on ourselves and on those whom we love. When we die, our loved ones will trace this holy sign on us for the last time.

In the name of the Father,
and of the Son,
and of the Holy Spirit. Amen.

The Lord's Prayer

The Lord's Prayer, or the Our Father, is a very important prayer for Christians because Jesus himself taught it to his disciples, who taught it to his Church. Today, we say this prayer as part of Mass, in the Rosary, and in personal prayer. There are seven petitions in the Lord's Prayer. The first three ask for God to be glorified and praised, and the next four ask for God to help take care of our physical and spiritual needs.

Our Father, who art in heaven,
hallowed be thy name;
thy kingdom come,
thy will be done
on earth as it is in heaven.
Give us this day our daily bread,
and forgive us our trespasses,
as we forgive those who trespass against us;
and lead us not into temptation, but deliver us from evil.

The Apostles' Creed

The Apostles' Creed is one of the earliest creeds we have; scholars believe it was written within the second century. The Apostles' Creed is shorter than the Nicene Creed, but it states what we believe about the Father, Son, and Holy Spirit. This prayer is sometimes used at Mass, especially at Masses with children, and is part of the Rosary.

I believe in God,
the Father almighty,
Creator of heaven and earth,
and in Jesus Christ, his only Son, our Lord,
who was conceived by the Holy Spirit,
born of the Virgin Mary,
suffered under Pontius Pilate,
was crucified, died and was buried;
he descended into hell;
and on the third day he rose again from the dead;
he ascended into heaven,
and is seated at the right hand of God the Father almighty;
from there he will come to judge the living and the dead.

I believe in the Holy Spirit,
the holy catholic Church,
the communion of saints,
the forgiveness of sins,
the resurrection of the body,
and life everlasting. Amen.

The Nicene Creed

The Nicene Creed was written at the Council of Nicaea in 325 AD, when bishops of the Church gathered together in order to articulate true belief in who Christ is and his relationship to God the Father. The Nicene Creed was the final document of that Council, written so that all the faithful may know the central teachings of Christianity. We say this prayer at Mass.

I believe in one God,
the Father almighty,
maker of heaven and earth,
of all things visible and invisible.
I believe in one Lord Jesus Christ,
the Only Begotten Son of God,
born of the Father before all ages.
God from God, Light from Light,
true God from true God,
begotten, not made, consubstantial with the Father;
through him all things were made.
For us men and for our salvation
he came down from heaven,
and by the Holy Spirit was incarnate of the Virgin Mary,
and became man.

For our sake he was crucified under Pontius Pilate,
he suffered death and was buried,
and rose again on the third day
in accordance with the Scriptures.

He ascended into heaven
and is seated at the right hand of the Father.
He will come again in glory
to judge the living and the dead
and his kingdom will have no end.

I believe in the Holy Spirit, the Lord, the giver of life,
who proceeds from the Father and the Son,
who with the Father and Son is adored and glorified,
who has spoken through the prophets.

I believe in one holy, catholic, and apostolic Church.
I confess one Baptism for the forgiveness of sins
and I look forward to the resurrection of the dead
and the life of the world to come. Amen.

Glory Be (Doxology)

This is a short prayer that Christians sometimes add to the end of psalms. It is prayed during the Rosary and usually follows the opening verse during the Liturgy of the Hours. It can be prayed at any time during the day.

Glory be to the Father

and to the Son

and to the Holy Spirit,

as it was in the beginning

is now, and ever shall be

world without end. Amen.

Hail Mary

The first two lines of this prayer are the words of the angel Gabriel to Mary, when he announces that she is with child (Luke 1:28). The second two lines are Elizabeth's greeting to Mary (Luke 1:42). The last four lines come to us from deep in history, from where and from whom we do not know. This prayer is part of the Rosary and is often used by Christians for personal prayer.

Hail, Mary, full of grace,

the Lord is with thee.

Blessed art thou among women

and blessed is the fruit of thy womb, Jesus.

Holy Mary, Mother of God,

pray for us sinners,

now and at the hour of our death.

Amen.

Grace before Meals

Families pray before meals in different ways. Some families make up a prayer in their own words, other families sing a prayer, and many families use this traditional formula. Teach your children to say this prayer while signing themselves with the cross.

Bless us, O Lord, and these thy gifts,

which we are about to receive from thy bounty,

through Christ our Lord.

Amen.

Grace after Meals

Teach your children to say this prayer after meals, while signing themselves with the cross. The part in brackets is optional.

We give thee thanks, for all thy benefits,

almighty God, who lives and reigns forever.

[And may the souls of the faithful departed,

through the mercy of God, rest in peace.]

Amen.

Celebrating Sunday for Catholic Families 2016–2017

by Patricia J. Hughes

This resource provides an approachable way for families to integrate Sunday Mass into their lives.

The following materials are provided for each Sunday:

- Gospel reading and reflection
- Discussion questions
- Suggested family activity

"Using this tool is a great way to help the family share at a deeper level about the Liturgy of the Word, naturally incorporating the Word into family conversation."

— Esther S. Hicks,
Director of Catholic School Identity and Mission,
Office of Catholic Schools, Archdiocese of Chicago

"The readings, reflections, activities, and prayers . . . will help the children to better understand, love, and live Sunday Mass."

— Maruja Sedano,
Director, Office for Catechesis and Youth Ministry,
Archdiocese of Chicago

ISBN 978-1-61671-263-1
50500
9 781616 712631
CSCF17
$5.00